P:

The

By

Copyright©2013 9, Dec 2013-2015 African-Y'sra'el
International Qahalim – Second Edition

Revised: 23, Feb 2015

Rebbe Simon Altaf, email: shimoun63@yahoo.com
Rebbe Lamont Clophus, African-Israel, 8111 Mainland, Suite 104-152, San Antonio, Texas, 78240, USA

1

For Africa: Contact us

Gulf: Rabbi John 971 244 63 617

Philippines: Rabbi Robert: 63-908-444-2866

North America Chief Rabbi: Rabbi Kefa Ben Yahudah
Tel: 1-210-827-3907

Visit our website at: www.african-israel.com

Youtube channel: www.youtube.com/simalt or visit our website above.

Visit our website at: www.african-israel.com

All quotes are from the Hidden Truths Hebraic Scrolls.

All quotes are from the Hidden-Truths Hebraic Scrolls unless otherwise stated. We encourage you to buy these scriptures from the above website or www.amazon.com.

Cautious note
Rebbe Simon Altaf Hakohen does not believe Yahushua is rebbe Yeshua. However the information is presented as is regards Christian doctrines. Torah is king and should be adhered to, there is no greater revelation. Tanak is the only sacred book available to us to run our lives and live according to the Halacha, set by our elders. The only accepted form of salvation is found in the books of the Torah, which is to adhere to the G-d of Israel and his voice which are the contracts he gave for us to obey. Get our Hidden-Truths Hebraic Scrolls Tanak for more understanding on the matter.

Preface

If I asked you to tell me what is the difference between secular and sacred text what would your answer be?

Most of you will say that sacred text is under the inspiration of the Em Chokmah or the Holy Spirit.

> **We'Yikra (Lev) 10:10** And that **you** may distinguish between **set-apart** and **not set-apart**, and between clean and unclean.

While many people out there would not even know how to classify a text as secular or sacred. The criterion to define sacred text is not whether it is Holy Spirit inspired. Anyone can claim they have received a text inspired by the Holy Spirit so would that then just classify as sacred even if it contradicts earlier revelations or maybe it does not contradict at all? What about a dictionary that presents history quite accurately would that then be classified sacred and inspired?

So if you read the verse from the Torah in Leviticus 10:10 carefully then G-d has adjudged us the Lewites, the Kohanim to decide what is sacred and what is not. Sorry not the Holy Spirit that is a Christian deception fostered on the people. The physical priesthood had the charge to do that leaving no doubt as to secular or sacred for the immediate Hebrew people.

There are 3044 statements of "Thus saith the Lord" or Koh Umar YHWH, which is to say "Thus says YHWH" in Hebrew in the Tanak yet not a single one in the so called New Testament, the Brit ha Chadasha because none of it is sacred, the gentiles had a hayday corrupting it with their poison pen.

The challenge for you is to show a single statement in the New Testament of "Thus Says YHWH" for those of you who hold it sacred to prove me wrong? I as a Lewite set the challenge and am waiting to be proven wrong.

Your first problem; the truth is that not a single book of the NT has any such statement. So what would you do now?

Your second problem; The NT was not compiled into a single 27 volume book until 325 CE and there after by the Romans. So by Christendom's ignorant standard we Y'sra'el have to rely on the NT for Salvation/Rescue? This is not only ludicrous but atrocious. This means for over 1900 years they had no access to salvation from Abbah YHWH prior to the NT. The time from the Exodus to the time of the NT is roughly 1900 years.

Your third problem; Not a single biological Hebrew Rabbi attended the conference at Nicea organized by Constantine the Roman pagan king in 325 CE who called the New Testament a document sacred by his pagan pastors and Greek Bishops while clearly they needed the testimony of Lewites to make it sacred. Not a single Lewite was present to make the case.

In fact even the name of the Yeshua/Jesus, which became known as Jesus H Christ comes from Mithra, the Indian G-d Krishna and Jupiter's mixing together. The term Christ emerged from Greek G-ds and the Indian Krishna so they christened Jesus H Christ what it has become today, not even the real name of the alleged Messiah. Dropping the H for Horus later.

> At the Council of Nicaea, Constantine gathered together all the "presbyters" (pagan priests) of his day and all their G-ds and saviors and had them debate together in an attempt to create one composite "G-d" they all would agree to worship. This new "G-d" would be given all the combined attributes and basic life stories of their G-ds rolled into one. The list of G-ds represented by their respective "priests" included Eastern and Western G-ds and G-ddesses: Jove, Jupiter, Salenus, Baal, Thor, Gade, Apollo, Juno, Aries, Taurus, Minerva, Rhets, Mithra, Theo, Fragapatti, Atys, Durga, Indra, Neptune, Vulcan, Kriste, Agni, Croesus, Pelides, Huit, Hermes, Thulis, Thammus, Eguptus, Iao, Aph, Saturn, Gitchens, Minos, Maximo,

5

Hecla and Phernes and many more. (G-d's Book of Eskra, anon., ch. xlviii, paragraph 36). It was in this "context" that the "G-d" Jesus H. Christ was created. The long list was narrowed down to the main G-ds of the Roman Aristocracy (Zeus and the son of Zeus Apollo) and the G-ds worshipped by the bulk of the common people (Julius Caesar and the sun G-d Mithra) along with the Eastern G-d Krishna." -

"Constantine's intention at Nicaea was to create an entirely new G-d for his empire who would unite all religious factions under one deity. Presbyters were asked to debate and decide who their new G-d would be. Delegates argued among themselves, expressing personal motives for inclusion of particular writings that promoted the finer traits of their own special deity. Throughout the meeting, howling factions were immersed in heated debates, and the names of 53 G-ds were tabled for discussion. "As yet, no G-d had been selected by the council, and so they balloted in order to determine that matter... For one year and five months the balloting lasted..." (G-d's Book of Eskra, Prof. S. L. MacGuire's translation, Salisbury, 1922, chapter xlviii, paragraphs 36, 41)." -

"Julius Caesar (the initials JC and the name itself is very similar to Jesus Christ) was hailed as "G-d made manifest and universal Saviour of human life" as this new G-d would take on those same attributes i.e. G-d in the flesh, and his successor Augustus was called the "ancestral G-d and Saviour of the whole human race" (Man and his G-ds, Homer Smith, Little, Brown & Co., Boston, 1952)."

"At the end of that time, Constantine returned to the gathering to discover that the presbyters had not agreed on a new deity but had balloted down to a shortlist of five prospects: Caesar, Krishna, Mithra, Horus and Zeus (Historia Ecclesiastica, Eusebius, c. 325)." -

6

"To placate the powerful British factions he chose the great Druid G-d which was the sun G-d Hesus (an incarnation of Nimrood/Tammuz); To placate the faction from Egypt he chose the Assyrian sun G-d Horus (an incarnation of Nimrood/Tammuz); To placate the Eastern/Oriental factions he chose the Eastern Saviour-G-d, Krishna [Krishna is Sanskrit for Christ] (an incarnation of Nimrod/Tammuz)." -

Thus, 'Hesus - Horus - Khrishna' would by the official name of the new Roman G-d, which later became known as "Jesus H. Christ". A vote was taken and it was with a majority show of hands (161 votes to 157) that all three deities became one G-d.

"Following longstanding heathen custom, Constantine used the official gathering and the Roman apotheosis decree to legally deify two deities as one, and did so by democratic consent. A new G-d was proclaimed and "officially" ratified by Constantine (Acta Concilii Nicaeni, 1618). That purely political act of deification effectively and legally placed Hesus and Krishna among the Roman G-ds as one individual composite. That abstraction lent Earthly existence to amalgamated doctrines for the Empire's new religion; and because there was no letter "J" in alphabets until around the ninth century, the name subsequently evolved into 'Jesus Christ'." -

It is clear to me that you may have never paid attention to the questions I posed above and were given a lawless religion made by men from Rome to follow. Rome's g-d so to speak was Paul of Tarsus. He gave them enough ammunition beside the corruptions Rome added later in the New Testament as it was in their hands to give them some kind of religious authority but not by the G-d of Y'sra'el. However their own lying standards cannot stand the test of time.

Now if I asked you how can you be saved or rescued? What will you answer be in the 21st century?

7

Are you going to give me John 14:6 or John 3:15 or would you rather give me Romans 10:9? If you do then you have made a error as you do not understand the definition of sacred scripture. If I were to ask Moses the same question would he ask me to look at John 14:6, John 3:15 or perhaps Romans 10:9?

If I went to the Rebbe Yeshua would he say to me to go read John 14:6? This is the lie that you have bought wholesale, hook, line and sinker and yet many out there professing to be followers of rebbe Yeshua are nothing but sheep to the slaughter who do not live lawfully but live lawlessly without Torah. Not to say he is not even rebbe Yeshua but that is another issue they know nothing about.

As I suggested even the gospel of John did not circulate to all the synagogues in Y'sra'el in the time of John or Matthew and was never seen as sacred writ. Think about this for a moment and the historical sequence and significance. John was arrested soon after the death of Rebbe Yeshua in 30 CE. To read or keep or to pass it on. It certainly did not circulate like our modern newspapers in the first century, since there were people in Y'sra'el, who were hostile to the message. There was no round boy delivering the gospel of John to every synagogue with a copy given to the Temple.

This means John himself followed and obeyed the Torah strictly to the letter being of the House of Yahudah, he did not call Paul's letters sacred and neither did he call his own letters and account in his gospel sacred text either. Since the writer did not do that what right does it give you or the Roman clergy to decide on our people's behalf?

Now what about John 14:6 and 3:15? Its totally misunderstood and misapplied text by Christendom. You will be happy to know that it is not what Christendom has been teaching you all this time. They have merely preached a falsehood, while the message in that verse is about keeping the Torah of Moses. That message they never preached even once. For that they will receive judgement.

Their G-d is not their ethnically white Jesus Christ but Paul who I call their lesser G-d who they keep talking about and quoting. By the way the alleged Messiah was black and his name was not Jesus H Christ either!

So this brings us back to what is sacred and what is secular and this question will keep being asked until the correct and true answer is given. Who decides when we call a text sacred? Well if you call the NT sacred then the decision was made for you by the gentile Catholics. However not as far as we the Hebrew Lewites are concerned, we do not hold to a gentile institution that is devoid of truth and give it any such authority. The only sacred text that G-d has given us through the hands of the prophets is the Tanak (the Hebrew Bible). Anything after that classes into history and secular which is very simple for us to understand. The Lewites had the position to decide the difference between <u>clean (sacred)</u> and <u>unclean (secular)</u> (Leviticus 10:10) so the hammer has struck for us and we already know. Even Musa said the following about us:

> **Debarim (Deut) 33:8-9** And of Lewi he said, Let your Thummim and your Urim be with your favoured one, whom You did prove at Massah, and with whom You did strive at the mayim of Meribah; **9** Who said to his father and to his mother, I have not seen him; neither did he acknowledge his brethren, nor knew his own children: **<u>for they have observed your word, and kept your Contract/Agreement</u>**.

The House of Lewi was tested and proven to be faithful. They did not care about their wayward brethren, they did not care even if it were their parents nor did they care if their wives and children rebelled against them but they were sincere and faithful followers of YHWH's Torah. Look what happened when Zipporah rebelled against Moses the Lewi, she was sent packing back to her father (Exo 18:2). Moses took decisive action, while many of you today cannot decide what to do with your rebellious spouses and allow the rebellion to rob you of shalom in your homes! She was duly returned after being corrected by her father as was custom.

9

Debarim (Deut) 21:5 And the kohenim the sons of Lewi shall come near; for them YHWH Your POWER has chosen to speak to him, and to Benefit in the name of YHWH; and **by their word shall every controversy and every stroke be tried**:

It says by their "word" every controversy shall be settled, that is the Lewite kohanim, and not a Pastor or Bishop who are clueless in our scrolls.

Therefore this Lewite Kohen Simon Altaf writing this book states clearly that Paul and his texts are not sacred and not halakik and neither are any other books of the NT. If the NT is to be observed it must look back to the Torah for all the laws, commandments and statutes. Anything that contradicts in the NT should be thrown out, unfortunately most of it does. When the goyim (gentiles) begin to understand this basic formula they will realize the monumental fraud committed upon them by their gentile forefathers. So today I submit to you Paul the wolf that is described in a prophecy in the scroll of Beresheeth (Genesis) in our Torah.

Beresheeth (Gen) 49:27 Benyamin is a **ravenous wolf**: in the morning he shall devour the prey, and at night he shall divide the spoil.

This prophecy is about the alleged Apostle Paul who is described as a RAVENOUS WOLF! Sadly this part was to be played by one of our own and its prophetic.

What is a wolf's job? The wolf is a highly monogamous creature that is directly the allegorical depiction of Satan. He will remove you from the Torah where the laws of YHWH are paramount and he will put you in the laws of the gentiles. So from Torah marriage you will end up with gentile serial monogamy. From right-ruling you will end up with lawlessness. From peace you will end up in chaos. From benefits you will end up in curses.

Now examine your life which of these is evident. Then ask yourself, what is Paul and his teachings done to you. If they

10

take on any higher meaning then the above mentioned curses mentioned in the Torah in the pages of Deut 27 and 28 will come upon you.

The question is not whether he did it deliberately or ignorantly was he or was he not trying to remove people from the Torah. His letters are not inspired and he is one of the false Apostles spoken about in the same NT Rev 2:2. That is a crushing blow to the man-made religion called Christianity, which mixes paganism with some truth.

> **Revelation 2:2** I know your works, and your labour, and your patience, and how you cannot tolerate them which are evil: and you have tried them which said **they are Emissaries**, and are not, and have found them liars:

Many people came who claimed to be apostles but were caught out teaching false doctrines and have no allegiance to Y'sra'el or her maker. They were found liars because they erected their own denominations and gave themselves new names but had no reality of the truth of the belief that was given to Y'sra'el. They did not obey the Torah. A certain person called Paul, who wrote twelve letters is also accused of this as by his own admission in Asia Minor including the Ephesians ALL rejected him. There were many Jews in these places and they knew the Torah well, they would not reject someone who came to teach them the Torah but you dare try to tell them stop circumcising, stop doing the things the Torah commands you then you will see the wrath they will have upon you as they did towards Paul.

Second Timothy 1:15 is the personal testimony of that person.

> **Second Timothy 1:15** This you know, that **all they which are in Asia Minor (Turkey) deserted me**; of whom are Phygellus and Hermogenes.

Paul's own testimony to say that he was rejected in Ephesus. So this is how the whole case is setup.

11

Here rebbe Yeshua gives congratulation to the Ephesians who have tried these false apostles such as Paul and rejected them.

> **Revelation 2:2** I know your works, and your labour, and your patience, and how you cannot tolerate them which are evil: and you have tried them which said **they are Emissaries** and are not and have found them liars:

So next time you raise up Paul be very careful to what you say and how you say it. Many claim to do miracles from reading Paul's letters but I submit to you today that even people have been able to do and receive miracles that only had the Muslim holy book called the Qur'an. Miracles are not match to the trust and obedience to the Torah that is required.

Chapter 1
An open examination of Paul and his claims

Acts 7:58 And cast him out of the city, and stoned him: and the witnesses laid down their clothes at a young man's feet, whose name was Sha'ul. **59** And they stoned Tsephan'yah (Stephen), calling upon G-d, and saying, Yahushua receive my ruakh (spirit).

We first hear about the character of Paul, here called by his real Hebrew name Sha'ul as a young man. One must understand here the definition of young is not our modern designation but in the ancient times, when a man was thirty years of age, that is what was young. Paul is described as a man in his thirties. He was working for the Sanhedrin who according to him did not want to hear anything about Yahushua as the alleged Messiah since Caiaphas had through false witnesses had him executed by putting on the tree. These are the words of the gospels and not mine. Thought Caiaphas unfortunately has been implicated in some things wrongfully.

Mattityahu 26:57-65 And they that had laid hold on Yahushua led him away to **Qayapha the Kohen Ha Gadol** (High Priest), where the experts of the Torah and the elders were assembled. **60** But they did not find anything against Him: yet, many false witnesses came. At the end two came forward, **61** And said, This fellow said, I am able to destroy the Beyth HaMikdash (Temple) of G-d, and to build it in three days. **62** And the Kohen Ha Gadol (High Priest) arose, and said to him have you no answer? What is this that they are testifying against you? **63** But Yahushua held his shalom. And the Kohen Ha Gadol (High Priest) answered and said to him, I put you under oath by the living G-d, that you tell us whether you be rebbe Yeshua, the Son of G-d. **64** Yahushua said to him, You have said it yourself, nevertheless I say to you, Hereafter you shall see the Son of Man sitting on the

13

right hand of Power,[1] and coming in the clouds of shamayim. **65** Then the Kohen Ha Gadol (High Priest) tore his clothes, saying, **He has spoken blasphemy; what further need have we of witnesses**? Behold, now you have heard his blasphemy.

They were the ones who had rebbe Yeshua through false charges of blasphemy, they were the ones who had rebbe Yeshua killed. Once again Tsephan'yah (Steven) was being stoned to death for a charge of blasphemy according to the book of Acts chapter 6 to 7:59. There is only one problem, the man allegedly claimed to be Caiaphas was never a High Priest. This indicates that this is a false charge brought against the High priest to deliberately slander him, no doubt by the gentiles.

Paul was standing there as an innocent bystander if you like.

Tsephan'yah was not just stoned by a mob as many think but with a proper council there that sat and judged him as a blasphemer.

> **Acts 6:12** And they stirred up the people, and the elders, and the experts in the Torah, and came upon him, and seized him, and brought him to the Sanhedrin, **13** And set up false witnesses, which said, This man ceases not to speak against this set-apart place,[2] and the Torah. **14** For we have heard him say, that this Yahushua of Netzer'eth shall destroy this place, and shall change the customs which Musa has handed to us.

As can be seen the Sanhedrin which was a court of seventy judges plus one equals seventy one judges or Rabbis who were elders sat in the court. The entire Sanhedrin did not sit however the council that sat had ruled on a alleged charge. Allegedly Yahushua had died and already risen. He did not come to destroy the Temple, the very institution where the Shekinah of G-d dwelled. Even though such a charge was

---

[1] First century idiomatic expression for YHWH.
[2] The Temple, note all believers were Torah practisers.

14

brought against Stephen through the council but Caiaphas was not the High Priest. This shows me that Roman Scribes have been deliberately deceptive to deceive the masses and most of you have believed it. Caiaphas whose real name was Yosef, his patronym was struck off from the gospels so people could not recognise him but fortunately for us we have available to us some records to know. The same with the other gospels patronyms removed so you cannot find out who is John, Mark, Matthew or Luke. You may be surprised to know all the gospels have been coloured and the letters of John and Peter are a total fraud. They did not speak fluent street Greek nor write in Hebrew so unless you want to believe they lived in Athens opposed to the North of Israel you are living in deception land.

In order to have Steven killed two witnesses had to be present. These witnesses were setup by Paul himself who stood there innocently allegedly. So what does that make him? A person who advances falsehood and is an accomplice!

Only one issue, the High Priest Caiaphas could not have ordered this death as they were not permitted to put people to death but had to hand them to the Romans. This is how we know the book of Acts is full of falsehoods and baseless testimony of gentiles claiming to be Hebrew.

What you sow you reap also.

> **Acts 23:12** And when it was day, certain of the Yahudim conspired together, and bound themselves under an oath, saying that they would neither eat nor drink till they had killed Paul.

The same murderer allegedly Paul was also going to be killed by his own fellows when he turned against them. So we read.

> **Acts 7:55-56** But he, being full of the Ruakh Ha Kadosh (Set-Apart Spirit), looked up steadfastly into shamayim, and saw the esteem of G-d, and Yahushua standing on the right hand of G-d, 56 And said,

15

Behold, I see the shamayim opened, and the Son of Man standing on the right hand of G-d.

This was the blasphemy in that Tsephan'yah had called this Son of Man the "G-d of Y'sra'el" and an equal to the Father in the Shaymayim (Heavens) in principle but this was unacceptable to the people standing there. It is actually true if it happened, we are not permitted to receive a G-d/man Messiah. This is how the deception been weaved.

> **Acts 7:57-58** Then they cried out with a loud voice, and stopped their ears, and ran upon him with one accord, **58** And cast him out of the city, and stoned him: and the witnesses laid down their clothes at a young man's feet, **whose name was Sha'ul**.

So they with the consent of the Sanhedrin (impossible as the Sanhedrin did not have the authority to put someone to death) took Tsephan'yah to stone him to death outside the city as the city was seen to be the camp of the faithful and so he had to be de-camped so to speak and killed outside the camp not to be bring blood guilt on the city.

Unfortunately Christendom in its ignorance has made out Paul to be higher than G-d. Everything that he said which is contradictory to the Rebbe Yeshua seems to be held even above the the Father's word. This is the blasphemy that is being committed by Christendom now and in past times since their inception, which started with this murderer Paul. So if your leader is a murderer then what does it make you the one who follows such a leader?

If one was to follow the written Torah you would not have any part of a murderer. This is why the history of Christendom is a bloody history and not a nice one. Need I remind you what the crusades were about and how they went and murdered many innocent people along the way on their conquest to free Jerusalem. Many people were murdered of all ethnicities especially Jews. The real Jews were not your typical Ashkenazim, who are converts from Khazaria, however they are mostly Torah keeping so they will get their just rewards from Hashem. The real chosen seed were people of black colour. See my book, Yahushua, the Black Messiah and Beyth Yahushua, the Son of Tzadok, the Son of Dawud.

Now coming back to Paul how did he get so close to the Sanhedrin and who was he?

We hear of a person mentioned in the (NT) called Nicodemus, he was a very rich grain and Jar trader in Jerusalem. He was also the teacher of the Torah in the Temple.

> **John 3:1** There was a man of the Pharisees, named Nakdimon (Nicodemus), a ruler of the Yahudim:

We are not told in the (NT) what relationship Sha'ul had with Nicodemus. Both of these were from the tribe of Benjamin. This means they were of the same clan but Nicodemus was a right-ruling man and had no personal agendas.

> [3]Paul who calls Miriam his sister in (Col 4:10) that would be a cousin/sister and I would suggest that Sha'ul would be the nephew of Nicodemus. We are given another clue that Bar'nabah was in Cyprus and of Lewite stock. Well what was Bar'nabah doing in Cyprus?

> Cyprus would be an important place for the trade of Tin and metal and we know that Yosef of Arimathaea was trading in that field both in the UK and probably sailing to Cyprus and Turkey also which was the closest location for trading of these metals.

> Using the rules of kinship analysis (For these rules see Lewis Morgan, Bronislaw Malinowski and Ernest L. Schusky) of ruling tribes of Africa and Israelites which connect back to their African ancestors such as Enoch known as Nok in that land and Noah (Bor-Nu the land of Noah in Africa) whose ark floated around Lake Chad

---

[3] Beyth Yahushua, the Son of Tzadok, the Son of Dawud page 103-104

bordering Nigeria landing close by Mount Meru (see for more Dr. David M. Westley on his African studies) (Meni in the Bible) note it used to be a sea. We find that using the rules of kinship pattern like his forefathers Yosef of Arimathaea would have more than one wife as was custom in the Ysraelites.

Nicodemus also in the same pattern would have had two wives in the north and south axis. How do we know this? This is because Nicodemus's wife named her eldest son the name Eli'ezer and that was a grandfather in the line of Nicodemus's wife.

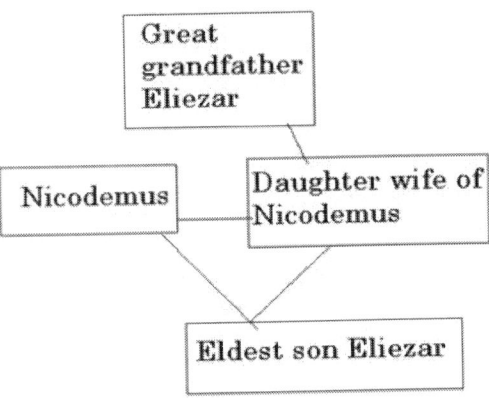

The name of the grandfather indicates to us that this is the same ruler pattern we find in Genesis with three sons and two wives. This pattern can be noted in Genesis 4, 5 and further on.

The kinship pattern is first clearly revealed by Lamekh but followed in all the future generations later but who killed and suppressed this pattern? Christendom of course with their half truths.

Genesis 4:19, 22 And Lamekh took unto him two wives: the name of the one was Adah, and the name of the other Zillah. 22 And Zillah, she also bare TubalQayin, an instructor in every instrument of brass and iron: and the sister of TubalQayin was Naamah.

18

The fact that Zillah has given the name TubalQayin to her son is evident that the pattern is running in these families of the North and South Axis. TubalQayin's name is identical to his father while the name means "metal worker" we can see that Zillah was Lemekh's wife from the Father's side so she names her firstborn after the grandfather. The Torah says that Qayin went to the land of Nod that is the land of Nok in Nigeria where he started his family. This is where we find the Nok culture.

This gives us better understanding now what we are dealing with.

The test of a True prophet of YHWH.

> **Deut 13:1-4** If there arise among you a prophet, or a dreamer of dreams, and gives you a sign or a miracle comes to pass, 2 And the sign or the miracle that came to pass, about which he spoke to you, saying, Let us go after other powers, which You have not known, and let us serve them; 3 You shall not listen to the words of that prophet, or that dreamer of dreams: for YHWH Your POWER is testing you, to know whether you love YHWH Your POWER with all your heart and with all your soul. 4 You shall keep the halacha (commandments) of YHWH Your POWER, and fear him, and guard His commandments, and obey his voice, and you shall serve him, and cling to him.

Anyone who teaches against the Torot/laws of YHWH is guilty of a transgression and cannot be trusted as a prophet. Paul fits this category by his own admission in his writings.

> **Galatians 3:19** (KJV) Wherefore then serveth the law? It was added because of transgressions, till the seed should come to whom the promise was made; and it was ordained by angels in the hand of a mediator.

YHWH has not stated anywhere that law was added in other words Paul's writing in Galatians is based on presumption. There was something else in place and one day G-d decided

19

and said I must add the Torah while historically even Chanok (Enoch) had the Torah, now explain how Chanok not only had the Torah but taught it to all the Kings of Africa for 243 years.

> **Yashar 3:12** And Chanoch reigned over the sons of men **two hundred and forty-three years**, and he did justice and right-ruling with all his people, and he led them in the halachot of YHWH.

(Question) When did YHWH gave the law by angels?

In Exodus 19:19 He directly came down to give the Torah and angels did not utter it. Angels may have been present with YHWH but they were not the givers of the Torah.

Furthermore, Paul makes the claim that G-d added the law for transgression. This would imply that another law was in place before that. Since angels had to be judged by something different when they fell if it was presumably added for transgression later makes no sense. This is the falsehood of Paul and Christendom today since by definition G-d's voice is his law/Torah. Otherwise it would imply G-d had no voice.

Paul subsequently makes a claim directly against the Torah in Galatians 3:19

> Gal 3:19 (KJV) Wherefore then serveth the law? It was added because of transgressions, till the seed should come to whom the promise was made; and it was ordained by angels in the hand of a mediator.

The KJV makes it clear the word "until" the seed comes in which the Christians then arrive at the faulty conclusion that after rebbe Yeshua, there is no need for the Torah.

Gal 3:19 Why then was the Torah given? It was added because of transgressions, so the seed should come to whom the promise was made; and it was appointed by malakhim in the hand of a mediator.

20

Gal 4:8 Formerly, when you did not know YHWH, you were enslaved by false G-d. 9 But now, after that you have known YHWH, and have knowledge of YHWH, how come you turn again to the weak and poor principles, do you desire again to be enslaved by them?

Paul implies in Galatians 4:9 that the principles of Torah are weak and poor. This is his biggest mistake.

Questions: What value do we give the personal testimony of Paul of being an Apostle? Luke is the only person who called him an Apostle or a "witness" only once in Acts 14:14.

Gal 1:7 Paul claims to have gone into Arabia but Luke makes no such claim.

In the Arabic version it says he went to Balcam which is a city in Syria and not Arabia. It makes no sense that Paul would go to Arabia since he was already in Syria then why would he go to Syria when he was in Syria. The only place in Arabia where he could have gone to is the Mount of Sinai and that was very far away from him and he makes no direct reference to going there.

According to Galatians 1:18 it was after three years he went to Jerusalem and then he met Peter (Shimon Kefa) who then trained him for 15 days but Paul instead makes the claim that no one taught him. He even denies giving credit to his Torah teacher, who taught him Torah.

Remember no other disciple attests to any of this account. The question is where is the second witness? There isn't any.

If Paul was commissioned then why did he not immediately go to Jerusalem? Why wait three years? Does this sound right and the elders (council) were in Jerusalem. You would have to go to Jerusalem as per the command to the three festivals annually such as Unleavened Bread, Pentecost and Tabernacles.

21

If he was already a learned Pharisee, why would he need to go and study first? Study what exactly?

Even the story that Luke tells of Paul's vision, Luke was not an eye witness of that appearing of Rebbe Yeshua, he was only telling you what Paul had told him. That is not an eye witness account. It is like saying Paul told me I bought an ice cream so I am telling you Paul bought an ice cream though I did not witness him going to the shop or purchasing the ice cream. This is an extremely poor witness. In other words Luke as a Levite is protecting himself. Lewites do that at times but reserve Judgment for later.

Peter gave a real blow to Paul just saying he is just another brother and actually criticized him, if anyone can see it. Shimon Kefa was wise by doing that he did two jobs, removing Paul from his lofty title of Apostle and telling people to be careful of his theologies. However the letter of I, II Peter is not even authentic so who knows what has been added and removed. Likewise the letters of 1, 2, 3 John the same.

It was an indirect rebuke and caution to all believers at the time and later.

> **Second Peter 3:15-18** And account that the longsuffering of our Master for rescue; even as our beloved brother Paulos (Sha'ul) also according to the wisdom given to him has written to you; 16 As also in all his letters, speaking in them of these things; in which are some things hard to understand, which they that are undiscipled and unstable4 pervert, as they do also the other writings, to their own destruction. 17 You therefore, beloved, seeing you know these things before, beware lest you also, being led away with the error of the wicked, fall from your own steadfastness. 18 But grow in favour, and in the knowledge of our Master and Saviour Yahushua Messiah. To him be esteem both now and forever. Amein.

---

4 Shimon attacks Torah breakers who have been misled by Sha'ul who was not inspired nor a right-ruling teacher.

Peter admonishes finishing with follow the words of the Rebbe Yeshua.

The same story Paul told King Agrippa.

In Galatians 1:21 he himself says he went to Syria so it's likely he went to Syria and not Arabia.

Acts 22:21 says for Paul to depart from the Temple for fear of persecution and to be sent to the gentiles.

(Question) Note this is Paul telling his story. There was no mission apart from the mission to Y'sra'el so why send him to the gentiles? It contradicts Matthew 10:6 and Matthew 15:24 of what rebbe Yeshua said earlier. One could say if the rebbe was sending him to the House of Y'sra'el, who had become gentiles that is understandable but this was not the case here.

Shimon's second letter is a direct polemic against Paul if you have not recognized it.

Also Yaqub who is wrongly called James also wrote a polemic against Paul in his letter.

Notice how the two elders answered the Pauline heresy in the first century?

Paul was preaching a gospel devoid of Torah and therefore many were being led astray and this called into question the leadership who then chose to give an opinion and an answer to those who had the ears to listen.

Why did they not directly attack Paul? They decided it was unwise to confront Paul and whatever good work had been done would be derailed. They chose the wise option. It is wrong to slander people so they chose not to slander him publicly. Many would be wise to learn from this example.

It is all about the matter of time, even though sometimes we call people our brother in the faith but only time will tell if he/she really holds to that faith or falls away hence why they gambled with time and knew that those who will hold fast to the Torah would never accept the Pauline lies and they were right about that as if I can make that choice after two thousand years I am sure many of you can too.

I used to call a few people brothers but they turned out be liars.

Paul's lie

> Rom 4:2 (KJV) For if Abraham were justified by works, he hath whereof to glory; but not before G-d.

Jacob's (James) response:

> James 2:21 (KJV) Was not Abraham our father **justified by works**, when he had offered Isaac his son upon the altar?

The third elder John also admonished Paul's teachings of Docetism as errant.

"Many deceivers, who do **not acknowledge Yahushua as coming in human flesh** Greek, *Sarx*, human flesh, have gone out into the world. Any such person is the deceiver and the anti-Messiah." (Second John 1:7.)

John rebuked the teachings of Paul in Colossians 1:15-16

> **Col 1:15** Who is the image of the invisible G-d, the firstborn of every creature:

> **Col 1:16** For by him were all things created, that are in heaven, and that are in earth, visible and invisible, whether they be thrones, or dominions, or principalities, or powers: all things were created by him, and for him:

Using these teachings people like Marcion formed Docetism. Docetism teaches though rebbe Yeshua came in Human flesh but not really as it was pretend flesh and not really human.

Second Peter 2:1 directly refutes Paul's Docetism conclusions.

Second Peter 2:1 But there were false prophets also among the people, even as there shall be false teachers among you, who privately shall bring in damnable heresies, even denying the Master that bought them, and bring upon themselves swift destruction.

It does not stop here. Paul goes on to make many false statements such as G-d does not live in Temples. Acts 17:24.

This contradicts in Acts 2:46, 21:20–26 and 1 Cor. 10:18–19.

Did rebbe Yeshua say otherwise; yes read below.

> Mat 23:21 And who shall swear by the Beyth HaMikdash (Temple), swears by it, and **by Him that dwells therein.**

As I said earlier rebbe Yeshua an ordinary man not born through any virgin birth has been made into a G-d/man and its unfortunate that many people are led into avodah Zarah (idolatry). Its time to come out of that idolatry and walk the Torah as G-d demands.

Chapter 2
Paul the self repeated Apostle

Paul lips do not get tired calling himself an apostle yet a self appointed one.

> **Rom 1:1** (KJV) Paul, a servant of Jesus Christ, called *to be* an Apostle.

> **Rom 11:13** (KJV) For I speak to you Gentiles, inasmuch as I am the apostle of the Gentiles, I magnify mine office:

Why was Paul commissioned to be a preacher to the gentiles?

Who commissioned him?

Paul office of authority

Many in Christendom are running in circles and this includes the Messianic camp and those in the Torah groups that do not have revelation of the things of the G-d of Y'sra'el.

They usually will cite the following;

> **Eph 4:11** (KJV) And he gave some, apostles; and some, prophets; and some, evangelists; and some, pastors and teachers;

Paul claims that it was Rebbe Yeshua who gave these offices and Christendom is all about Deacons, Pastors and Bishops, etc, etc but the only trouble is where does Rebbe Yeshua make a single mention of having these offices? The title Pastor was used by Pagan worshippers to their false deities that will never stand. This was one of the key titles used by Constantine's clergy who proclaimed Christianity joining three G-ds into one, the G-d Krishna from India, who is known as Vishnu. His wife is Lakhsmi, the G-ddess of wealth and beauty.

Constantine used the druid G-d Hesus, he used the Egyptian and Assyrian G-d Horus. These are all incarnations of Nimrood and Tammuz, the symbol of the Christian cross comes from these false religions. Rebbe Yeshua did not hang on a cross but he was hung on a Tree (Deut 21:22 and Acts 5:30).

Thus Hesus Horus Krishna would be the official name of the new Roman G-d, which later became known as Jesus Christ.

The inscription of the new G-d was IHS which stood for Isis, Horus and Seb. Tammuz, the symbol of the Cross is what you find even today in all church buildings Roman or otherwise.

The word Krish, Krishna means Black. He was in the Hindu scheme believed as the second person of the Hindu trinity and he descended in mortal human form to save humanity. This is how the trinity of Christianity came about in Rome after the events.

Paul's confusion and falsified statements that Christendom has taken to heart as some kind of proof and truth which really are Paul's own loose words adding pagan philosophies to them.

Does the Torah say that we can have these offices that the Pauline epistle describes? Should we not be going to the Torah to seek which offices are actually ordained versus this hodgepodge Pauline confusion?

Is the Torah not the Law and the place to go and look first? Is YHWH not going to use that for judgment? The answer is that He will use that to judge then it makes this the root and soul of everything.

Indeed it is, but little does Christendom recognize and realise it's error propagating falsehoods.

Do we find a single reference for the word "Pastor" given by Rebbe Yeshua in the gospels? Do we find Musa the greatest prophet to live, who took the children of Y'sra'el out of slavery to have said the same as Paul that these are the following

27

offices such as evangelists, pastors and teachers? Not in this order there is not.

There is no mention of this by Rebbe Yeshua in the gospels and no mention of it by Musa the greatest prophet to live. What about the word Evangelist? There is not a single mention of the word Evangelist in the gospels or either in the Torah.

The nearest you find in the KJV is in Acts 21:8 where allegedly Luke calls Philip an Evangelist mistranslated in the KJV, no surprises for guessing.

> **Acts 21:8** (KJV) And the next *day* we that were of Paul's company departed, and came unto Caesarea: and we entered into the house of Philip the evangelist, which was *one* of the seven; and abode with him.

The Greek term "yooang'ghelis'tace" Strong's G2099 is erroneous to be termed Evangelist. The best way to describe this is "proclaim" or "proclaimer" such as a herald.

Philip was actually a disciple of the rebbe Yeshua mentioned in Matthew 10:3.

> **Mattityahu 10:3 Philip**, and Bartholomi; Toma, and Mattityahu the tax collector; Yaqub the son of Alphaeus, and Lebai, whose surname was Theddai;

If Philip is a disciple would that then make him an evangelist? No. An Evangelist typically a herald of a king who would hold up a placard proclaiming something of his kingdom which the king instructed, like some new law or some act of punishment on someone. Philip did not hold any such placards saying first we were not saved but now we are saved. Such foolish theologies have no room in our Y'sra'elite walk.

While the context of Luke in Acts 21:8 is simply to show that he was proclaiming the arrival of rebbe Yeshua. What office did Rebbe Yeshua actually leave with his disciples, if he really did ascend?

28

Mattityahu 28:19-20 Go to them

20 And teaching them to **Guard and Do** [always applied to the Torah of Moses] all the words of the Commandments as a witness forever.

There were a few different endings of Matthew 28:-19-20.

Note in the <u>favoured</u> reading the rebbe tells them to "Go and teach." What would you be called if you taught others? A teacher, which is a Rabbi that is from the Torah what we classify as an elder. We call Musa Rebbenu, which is to mean "our teacher" or great one. The "Great" here does not make him greater than G-d but "great" in that he had the Torah explained to him and he wrote it down when he went to see YHWH upon the Mountain.

Which office does the Torah favour?

Let's put it another way what was Musa's office?

He was a prophet, Lewite, judge and King. Remember kings have to write the Torah and Musa wrote the Torah so he would be classified as a king technically.

And he then separated the roles by making Judges and Teachers in other words Lewites.

So what are the roles that the Torah identifies for us?

There are only four roles according to the Torah as follows;

1. Prophet,
2. Lewite/Rabbi (Teacher),
3. Judge
4. King

A Teacher can also be a Judge, prophet or a Rabbi. In the exile, the role that is missing from us is King. This is a role for later when we enter the land to be restored back when Messiah will be King born naturally.

So essentially we are allowed to make only use of two roles according to the Torah under the direction of our Rabbi.

Rabbi/Teacher
Judge

If you are a Lewite then you are automatically a teacher.

We do not make use of the prophet role as that is not someone that we train or a school trains but it's a role that ceased with the last three prophets Haggai, Zechari'yah and Malaki. Prophecy ceased long ago. The Abbah may restore this role just before we are ready to be restored back.

Let us go back and see what role Abraham had.

He was a prophet and a teacher.

> **Beresheeth (Genesis) 20:7** Now therefore restore the man's wife; for **he is a prophet**, and he will petition for you, and you will live: but if you do not restore her, know that you shall surely die, you, and all who are yours.

> **Beresheeth (Genesis) 12:5** Then Abram took Sarai his wife, and Lot his brother's son, and all their possessions that they had gathered, and **the people whom they had acquired in Kharan**; and they departed to go to the land of Kanan; so they came to the land of Kanan.

The people that Abraham had acquired came to him because he was **the teacher of the Torah** and these were the ones who had become the followers of YHWH.

What about Noakh?

He was a teacher as he and his son Shem had a Yeshivah or Beyth Midrash (House of Learning). Abraham went to them to study and so did Isaac and Jacob his son after him.

30

Yashar 9:5-6 And when Abram came out from the cave, he went to Noakh and his son Shem, and he remained with them to learn the instruction of YHWH and his ways, and no man knew where Abram was, and Abram served Noakh and Shem his son for a long time. 6 And Abram was in Noakh's house thirty-nine years, and Abram knew YHWH from three years old, and he went in the halachot of YHWH until the day of his death, as Noakh and his son Shem had taught him; and all the sons of the eretz in those days greatly transgressed against YHWH, and they rebelled against him and they served other G-d, and they forgot YHWH who had created them in the eretz; and the inhabitants of the eretz made unto themselves, at that time, every man his G-d; idols of wood and stone which could neither speak, hear, nor rescue, and the sons of men served them and they became their mighty ones.

Abraham had learnt the Torah from Noakh and Shem and was with them for thirty-nine years of his life. Not only did Abraham learnt the Torah but he was also kept safe there from Nimrood when Abraham was young he wanted to kill him.

What about Chanok?

He was a teacher but the African kings made him a prince over them so he was a kind of a judge or king over the kings.

What would be Adam's role?

He would also be a priest and a teacher. So a teacher is really an elder or a rabbi.

We have <u>no</u> roles such as Pastor or Evangelist. These are self created roles by gentile Christianity from the Pauline confusion and Paganism, the Pastor role was taken from gentile pagan religions. If you call yourself a Pastor I would encourage you to drop that title and use the more appropriate biblical term of Moreh for a teacher. A woman is a "morah". You also need to be teaching Torah and not the NT or Jesus is G-d idolatry.

So looking at Musa he was a judge and he enacted judgments.

Musa was the first king as well since he wrote the Torah and technically it makes him king also. However he quickly spread out the roles as was necessary.

So from this we can see that the roles that Paul claims to be offices of authority on which reams and reams of paper and ink has been wasted and continues to be wasted by Christendom and others is Paul's own opinion and not what he alleged rebbe Yeshua gave. Rebbe Yeshua gave no such offices. He told his disciples to go and teach the Torah so by definition they were elders/rabbis only. They chose within their ranks to make judges people like John Zabdi, Shimon Kefa and Yaqub who we were the first council mentioned in Acts 15 of the followers of rebbe Yeshua. This shows us within the disciples we find that all the roles apart from the role of prophet and king. This lines up perfectly with the four roles of Torah of Teacher, prophet, Judge and King.

Chapter 3
Paul the Apostle to the Gentiles

> **Romans 11:13 (KJV)** For I speak to you Gentiles, inasmuch as I am the **apostle of the Gentiles**, I magnify mine office:

There is no such office; no such commandment was given by Rebbe Yeshua. So where does Paul even get the idea it boggles one's mind? This is how he tried to squeeze himself in and deceive many people with his mishmash of contradictory teachings in his letters.

> **Matt 10:5** (KJV) These twelve Jesus sent forth, and commanded them, saying, **Go not into the way of the Gentiles**, and into *any* city of the Samaritans enter ye not:

By examining the above rebbe Yeshua said to his disciples for not to go to the gentiles or apply their way of gentile living to our Hebrew ways. In spite of this Christendom has been teaching a falsehoods, which is devoid of Torah and its precepts which are needed to be in the Contracts of YHWH to be rescued and redeemed are just not there.

> **Matthew 10:6** (HTHS) But go rather to the scattered sheep of the **Beyth Y'sra'el** (House of Y'sra'el: Ten tribes).

The scattered sheep of the Beyth Y'sra'el are the Y'sra'elites and not some gentiles waiting for rebbe Yeshua. The gentiles do not care about rebbe Yeshua and are happy to live in their atheistic hedonist lifestyles and should be left alone to do so.

The reason is simply the twelve tribes need to be gathered back. The earlier ousted Y'sra'elites into the Diaspora were to return back to Torah as that is what they had rejected and not to some new fad religion called Christianity, which simply teaches how to be lawless and has no part with us.

33

Hosea 5:15 I will go and return to my place, <u>**till they acknowledge their offence**</u>, and seek my face: in their affliction they will seek me early.

If rebbe Yeshua did everything then why do we have to go to Y'sra'el and repent for the transgressions of our forefathers? This means this is incumbent upon true Y'sra'elites still in spite of rebbe Yeshua, which only further exposes the fallacy of Christendom's lies.

Another false Christian dogma which has the least understanding of our way of life. The place where YHWH's name is today found in Tel Arad next to Beersheba, the only place in Y'sra'el where the name of YHWH was found historically. By the way one more thing ancient Y'sra'el's boundary also ran as far as Beersheba in Abraham's time. Further past that he would start entering the territory of the king of Gerar (Gen 20:1).

The real city of Dawud and his Tabernacle were/are in Tel Arad. This is the true Jerusalem of the Jebusites that King David conquered and the other Jerusalem where most of the people today go to is the Jerusalem of the Amorites but really none of the sites there are true.

We went to the true Jerusalem in 2014 in May to do the necessary repentance taking representatives from all three houses and we know YHWH accepted our Teshuvah to restore us back.

> **Hosea 6:1** (HTHS) Come, and <u>**let us return**</u>[5] to YHWH: for he has torn, and he will heal us; he has struck us, and he will bind us up.

Return where?

> **Debarim (Deut) 30:8** And You shall <u>**RETURN**</u> and obey the <u>**voice of YHWH**</u>, and <u>**do all his commandments**</u> which I command you this day.

---

[5] Efrayim ready to make repentance.

34

The only one place a transgressor is meant to return to after repenting is to the Torah but here since we transgressed YHWH's name in Y'sra'el we must return to Y'sra'el and do the repentance there.

YHWH commands us to return back to Torah, which is how we will be judged. We are not commanded to follow any books called New Testament or to put our faith in the corrupted books of the New Testament that Rome has had its hand in nor our faith in any man calling himself Jesus/Yeshua/Yahushua etc. The New Testament excluding Pauline epistles is simply a record of who rebbe Yeshua was and should be treated as such. They are not superior to the sacred text of the Tanak. The Torah is always king! Rebbe Yeshua was a man and not G-d/man.

We already know that books of the New Testament are tainted by gentile hands.

The Catholic Church admits of forgery of scriptures
The Catholic Encyclopaedia, Volume 6, page 136, gives us this admission. "Substitution of false documents and tampering with genuine ones was quite a trade in the Middle Ages. Innocent III (1198) points out nine species of forgery [of ecclesiastical records] which had come under his notice.

But such frauds of the Church were not confined to the Middle Ages; they begin even with the beginning of the Church and infest every period of its history for fifteen hundred years and defile nearly every document, both of "Scriptures" and of Church aggrandizement. As truly said by Collins, in his celebrated Discourse of Free Thinking:

Scripture according to Catholic Dogma is the New Testament which also is followed by the harlot Christianity. However as I said earlier not according to the lewitical standards and the laws and statutes and judgments given to us by the standard of Torah it is not.

35

So the question is did Paul's claims to be "Apostle of the gentiles" stand up in light of the references we have examined?"

The question can be answered in the negative that Paul's statement in light of the references cited do not hold up therefore his so called apostleship is only self proclaimed and contradictory to the evidence. You may then ask what about his testimony in the book of Acts? First that is not inspired but let's examine that as well shall we?

> **Acts 9:3-5** And as he journeyed, until he came near Dameshk (Damascus): and suddenly there shined round about him a light from the shamayim:
> **4** And he fell to the earth, and heard a voice saying to him, Sha'ul, Sha'ul, why do you persecute me?
> **5** And he said, who are you, Master? And the Master said, I am Yahushua whom you persecute.
> **6** And both trembling and astonished said, Master, what do you want me to do? And Rebbe Yeshua said to him, Arise, and go into the city, and it shall be told you what you must do.
> **7** And **the men who journeyed with him stood speechless, hearing a sound, but seeing no man**.

Here Paul claims that he was heading towards Damascus to bring the disciples of Rebbe Yeshua to the Sanhedrin in Jerusalem so they could be imprisoned under false charges. And while on the way he saw a light which startled him and from the light a voice issues that it was the voice of rebbe Yeshua but Paul saw no one. Apparently all the men with Paul saw the light and heard the voice but saw no man/image/thing according to verse 7.

First, the question is that G-d in the Tanak always revealed himself personally through the Angel of YHWH except on one occasion making a donkey speak (Numbers 22:28). Even on this occasion an animal was seen talking given the permission from the heavens. However why is it that when Paul receives his vision he sees nothing but a light? Why would rebbe

36

Yeshua who allegedly appeared to him not show himself personally? There is no reason for this visitation to be just light. Did you know behind the light is Satan as this happened to someone else too in Arabia who later proclaimed himself to be a prophet?

The verse in the King James Version Acts 9:5 said: *it is hard for thee to kick against the pricks.*

The only problem is that this bit of the text is not found in any earlier manuscript codex's so it has been added by a scribe of Rome. So what else did the scribe add to make Paul look true?

Then the following alleged claim:

> **Acts 9:15** But Yahushua said to him, Go your way: for he is a chosen vessel to me, to bear my name before the nation, and kings, and the children of Y'sra'el:

How come here a certain claim is laid but Yahushua made no such mention of this to his close twelve disciples. Even they were told not to go to the gentiles in Matthew 10:5 which now contradict the very words he told them?

So someone is telling a lie, either it is Paul or Luke. Clearly Luke is only writing what Paul is telling him so Paul is telling a lie and not Luke the Lewite. The other alternative is that a scribe took liberties to make amendments and this by the way was a common practice by gentile scribes.

In Acts 9:5-6, the words alleged to have spoken to Paul at the conversion were changed by scribes. This was done to harmonize them with the contradictions they contained with the text in Acts 26:14-15. The scribes also changed some readings of the book of Acts as you have one with shorter reading and one with longer reading.

It doesn't just stop there; let me show you more contradictions;

> **Acts 22:6-9** And it came to pass, that, as I made my journey, and was come near to Dameshk (Damascus)

37

about noon, suddenly there shone from the shamayim a great light round about me. **7** And I fell to the ground, and heard a voice saying to me, Sha'ul, Sha'ul, why do you persecute me? **8** And I answered, Who are you, Master? And he said to me, I am Yahushua of Netzer'eth, whom you persecute. **9** And **they that were with me saw indeed the light, and were afraid; but they heard not the voice** of him that spoke to me.

In Acts 9:7 it said that the men that were with Paul saw the light and heard the sound but in Acts 22:9 it says the men with him saw the light but heard <u>no</u> sound! This is a contradiction in the same book so which is it, sound or no sound. This shows someone tampered with the book and could not even reconcile the two accounts.

Paul was delusional and was duped by his own theologies. We have an account of a prophet in First Kings 13 where a prophet of YHWH was duped into believing another so called prophet who said YHWH had spoken to him while YHWH had not spoken at all. This cost this prophet who disobeyed YHWH his life.

First Kings 13:1, 14-18, 20, 21, 24 And, behold, there came a man of G-d out of Yahudah by the word of YHWH to Beyth'el: and Yarob'am stood by the altar to burn incense. **14** And went after the man of G-d, and found him sitting under a terebinth *tree*: and he said to him, Are you the man of G-d that came from Yahudah? And he said, I am. **15** Then he said to him, Come home with me, and eat lechem (bread). **16** And he said, I may not return with you, nor go in with you: neither will I eat lechem (bread) nor drink mayim with you in this place: **17** For it was commanded to me by the word of YHWH, You shall eat no lechem (bread) nor drink mayim there, nor turn again to go by the way that you came. **18** He said to him, I am a prophet also as you are; and a malakh spoke to me by the word of YHWH, saying, Bring him back with you into your house, that he may eat lechem (bread) and drink mayim. But he lied to him. **20** And it came to pass, as

38

they sat at the table, that the word of YHWH came to the prophet that brought him back: **21** And he cried to the man of G-d that came from Yahudah, saying, Thus says YHWH, Forasmuch as you have rebelled against the mouth of YHWH, and have not kept the commandment which YHWH Your POWER commanded you, **24** And when he was gone, <u>**a lion met him by the way, and slew him**</u>: and his carcass was cast in the way, and the donkey stood by it, the lion also stood by the carcass.

The moral of the story is quite clear don't listen to the likes of Paul who <u>will</u> take you away from the Torah to give you spiritual death.

Many have already fallen because they believed Paul due to his claims of having miracles in Second Corinthians 12:12 and Romans 15:19. However rebbe Yeshua had said that he will tell miracle doers in Matthew 7:21-23 that "I never knew You".

The Rebbe Yeshua warned in Matthew 24:26 to be on guard to those who say to you in the Desert here is rebbe Yeshua. Well Paul did claim he saw rebbe Yeshua in the Desert so the two statements correlate that you are to be careful of those claiming sights of the rebbe in the desert.

> **Matthew 24:26** Therefore if they shall say to you, Behold, he is in the wilderness; do not go: behold, he is in the inner rooms; do not believe it.

It's clear that the warning of the rebbe came true which is what Paul was uttering that he saw the rebbe in the Desert and leading people to a new Messiah in whom there is no Torah/Law and no more need of commandments.

The reality is that he was deceived because he did not see rebbe Yeshua but heard a voice and unless we believe Satan cannot speak the deception here was quite REAL.

39

No matter how much Pauline defenders defend him, he will remain a false teacher and a deceiver if these are his writings then he led people astray.

> **Galatians 5:2** Behold, I Paul say to ye, that if you be circumcised, Messiah shall profit ye nothing.

As can be seen by the so called letters of Paul he is telling people not to circumcise because if they do then rebbe Yeshua will profit them nothing. Well that is the literal reading of it. Now you can allegorize it as you like but this act alone is enough to bring Paul to the Jerusalem council for teaching against the Abrahamic Contract of circumcision by which we can enter that contract but if you are uncircumcised then you have no right to the contract. Therefore by what right Paul is teaching such a dogma is not only unprofitable but unwise and anti-Torah.

This can also be termed negation of the Torah/law. Did Paul teach it? Well you do not need to hear it from others just see what he wrote in Galatians 5:2, if these are his writings. I went to Kenya in 2013 and the elders there tried vehemently to defend Paul and said maybe I have gotten Paul mixed up but when I put the text of Galatians 5:2 in front of their faces then I saw them dancing around it to defend it but there is no defence for such false teachings in the community of Y'sra'el. And if the above is not enough let me show you more of his false teachings.

> **Galatians 5:3** For I testify again to each man that is circumcised, that he is a debtor to do the whole Torah.

One should ask plainly is that not what YHWH desired from us. The very reason why we got kicked out of our country was for not obeying the Torah and desecrating his name? So how could this be a bad thing?

> **Debarim (Deut) 28:1** And it shall come to pass, if You shall listen carefully to the voice of YHWH Your POWER, to Guard and to do <u>ALL his commandments</u>

40

which I command you this day, that YHWH Your POWER will elevate you high above all nations of the world:

Does not YHWH instruct and command us to do exactly the opposite of what Paul was teaching? Indeed any person who will read Debarim 28:1 will get to this conclusion and if you don't then I encourage seeing our history, why we were removed from our country and exiled.

Either way you go you cannot fight and twist the text of Galatians 5:1-3 and pretend it says something other than the obvious like the Kenyans leadership at Limuru who rejected the Torah in favour of foolish Pauline contradictions and dogma therefore we the true Y'sra'elite rejected them!

This soon followed by terrorist attack in Nairobi Kenya town where radical Muslims from al-Shabab attacked Westgate plaza and killed over 63 people and injured over 150. This was judgment from on high to reject the servants of YHWH who were there on 16th of August 2013 to teach the Torah, representatives from the House of Lewi and the House of Yahudah/House of Ephrayim, in Nairobi but were rejected as the natives would rather dance with Christianity and play their foolish drums so no one can hear the message of truth. They even had hailstones hit their building on the same day but the foolish gentile will remain foolish.

The same message of Torah was also taken to Ghana and there they accepted it and are benefitting from it right now as we speak the world is descending on Ghana for Gold and oil trade.

By the way the judgment is not finished here, more will come later to wake up the nation who sleep in slumber and think rejecting Torah is the answer to their problem. No it is the start of their problem. Every town in Kenya where the was rejected will be under a curse starting from Nairobi, to Kissi, to Narok. They are on a very short straw.

Galatians 5:4-6 Messiah is become of no effect to you,

41

whosoever of you is justified by the Torah; you are fallen from favour.

What the rebbe Yeshua and circumcision to do with anything this is the question one should ask? Rebbe Yeshua and circumcision are <u>mutually</u> exclusive so to link it with the rebbe Yeshua is an act of gross violation of Torah and Paul here is guilty of that by trying to justify his errant theology he attacks the Torah and its contracts. Christendom may believe this kind of nonsense but the Torah believers do not do any such thing and understand the contract of circumcision was given forever to perform. If I was given the choice to serve Abbah YHWH by circumcising and then asked do not circumcise and accept the Christian false Messiah, I would reject the false Messiah of Christendom and circumcise instead.

This is why I said if a Pharisee like Paul thinks he can remove circumcision in favour of his ill view he was quite mistaken for those who are filled by the Ruakh ha Kadosh (Holy Spirit) will uphold the commandment given in the Torah instead of his letters of no worth.

> **Galatians 5:5-6** For we through the Ruakh (Spirit) wait for the expectation of right-ruling <u>by belief</u>. **6** For in Yahushua **Rebbe Yeshua neither brit-milah <u>(circumcision) avails anything,</u> nor uncircumcision**; but belief which works through obedience.

The statement in the verse of Galatians 5:5-6 itself is both contradictory and misleading if anyone wishes to follow it then I will tell you that you have no part with Y'sra'el.

The "belief" that Paul was preaching was nothing but an <u>assent</u> of the mind which is not what the Y'sra'elites were to follow. They had a tangible belief in the Most High as they saw the Shekinah first hand, their forefathers had seen the fire and cloud and the evidence of judgments upon Egypt. There was no mistake on their part to put their "trust" in YHWH. They needed no airy fairy type gentile "belief" of the mind which is exactly what Christendom teaches today.

42

In this foolishness one is to believe in something in his "head only" and that somehow brings some kind of merit.

In verse 6 he tells you in Messiah circumcision will benefit you nothing. How dare he even say that? He has no right to contradict a covenantal agreement given by YHWH himself. Not Paul, not even rebbe Yeshua has the authority to annul what the Father has declared already.

> **Beresheeth (Gen) 17**:13 He who is born in your Beyth (house), and he who is bought with your money, must be circumcised; and My Contract/Agreement shall be in **your flesh for an everlasting Contract**/Agreement:

Who dares change this from EVERLASTING to temporal? No one dare do that and it is not permitted not to Paul and certainly not to Christendom's false ethnically white 'Jesus'. Rebbe Yeshua was ethnically Black, African looking. He taught everyone Torah and to obey it. Look at the following statement he made to the rich young ruler.

> **Matthew 19:16-17** And, behold, one came and said to him, **Rebbe, what Good mitzvoth (deeds) shall I do, that I may have eternal life**? **17** And he said to him, Why ask me concerning the good?[6] There is indeed one good, if you want to enter[7] into Life, **Guard and Do the commandments**.

As can be seen the rebbe Yeshua said words regarding the obedience to the Torah and the gentiles have ever since been disregarding and teaching false doctrines to the world in the guise of their foolish gospel.

All of you who follow this person Paul will fail and fall and remove benefits and increases from your life. As the Abbah YHWH said through the prophets the following is true as all

---

[6] The translation of the KJV here is incorrect. Yahushua is pointing to Torah observance which has the idiom for "good", used in PROV 4:2.
[7] The longer readings found in most Bibles are missing in the important manuscripts.

43

the right-ruling will obey the commandment to circumcise and the **lawless Torah breakers** will fall by the wayside.

> **Hosea 14:9** Who is wise, and he shall understand these things? Prudent and he shall know them? For the halachot (ways) of YHWH are right, and **the right-ruling shall walk in them**: but the **transgressors** shall fall therein.

Paul also fulfilled the prophecy of Matthew 5:19;

> **Matthew 5:19** Whoever therefore shall break one of the least of these commandments, and shall teach men to do so, he shall be called the LEAST in the kingdom of shamayim but whoever shall do and teach them, the same shall be called Rebbe (Great) in the kingdom of shamayim.

Paulo's Roman name would have been Pauxillus which mean "LEAST". So Paul would be known as the "Least" in the Kingdom. One may think that puts him inside the kingdom but actually it doesn't. It means those inside the kingdom who know of Paul will say this man is the "LEAST" for his deceptive teachings.

Paul's foolish teachings even brought a Greek into the Temple causing all sorts of local issues.

> **Acts 21:28-29** Shouting, Men of Y'sra'el, help: This is the man, that teaches all men everywhere against the people, and the Torah, and this place: and further brought Greeks also into the Beyth HaMikdash (Temple) inner courts, and has polluted this Set-Apart place. **29** (For they had seen before with him in the city Trophimos an Ephesian, whom they supposed that Paul had brought into the Beyth HaMikdash (Temple).)

In 58 CE a gentile student of Paul entered and violated the restriction set on the gentiles not to go beyond the area of the gentiles. This happened because Paul's contradictory teachings found in his letter to the Ephesians in 2:14-15 where

44

he taught the middle wall of partition is no longer in affect that the commandments are abolished. This caused an uproar in Jerusalem how his false teaching influenced Trophimus to do this.

This was also prophesied in Ezek 44:7 that a gentile would enter and defile the precinct.

>**Ezekiel 44:7** In that <u>you have brought into my sanctuary foreigners, uncircumcised in heart, and uncircumcised in flesh</u>, to be in my sanctuary, to pollute it, even my Temple, when you offer my Lakhem (bread), the fat and the blood, and they have broken my Contract/Agreement because of all your abominations.

This is another reason why Paul's bad teachings cannot be taken as serious doctrine and to be rejected. The Israelites were very careful to prevent any gentile going beyond the protective fence they had erected around the second Temple with a warning inscription declaring death to all the gentiles who dared to do so while clearly Trophimus was one who did not care nor think based on the faulty teachings of Paul. This is what happens when you ignorantly break Torah with the end result being death. Note also that Paul never defends the fact that Trophimus did not go into the Temple.

If you think this is bad enough there is more as gentile scribes took liberties to change text randomly as they desired. If some reading did not conform to their taste they amended it. Let me give you some proof.

>[8]Thus, to the statement in Col. 1.14 "in whom we have redemption, the forgiveness of sins," a few later Greek manuscripts add the words "through his blood," a phrase derived from the parallel in Eph. 1.7. (Here again the King James Version follows the secondary form of text.)

---

[8] Bruce Metzger on the textual criticism of the Bible.

45

1 Cor. 12.13, Paul declares "By one Spirit we were all baptized into one body . . . and all were made to drink of one Spirit." Several witnesses, however, conclude the statement thus: "all were made to drink of one drink,"

Further reading: Bruce M. Metzger & Bart D. Ehrman, "The Text of the New Testament: Its Transmission, Corruption, and Restoration", Oxford University Press New York, Oxford, 4 edition, 2005

Gospel of Matthew 16:2b–3 (the signs of the times), the passage describes a confrontation between Yahushua and the Pharisees and Sadducees over their demand for a sign from heaven. It is one of several passages of the New Testament that are absent from many early manuscripts. The authenticity of the passage has been disputed by scholars since the second half of the 19th century.

Chapter 4
Paul insisting he does not lie

Rom 3:7 For if by my lie the truth of G-d has more abounded through to his esteem; why yet am I also still judged as a sinner?

Paul has been claiming that he does not lie but then what are statements in his letters which are clear falsehoods.

The statement in Galatians 5:2 is a clear falsehood.

Galatians 5:2 Behold, I Paul say to ye, that if you be circumcised, Messiah shall profit ye nothing.

By denying the contract as everlasting this is a clear and utter falsehood in his letters. His pits his letters and he pit himself against the Torah and the disciples of rebbe Yeshua Yahushua and claims he is not lying but puts curses upon them.

In all of his letters he gave none of the teachings of rebbe Yeshua but spread his own lies and foolish Greek philosophies.

Where is the 13th self professed Apostle Paul in true Jerusalem.

Revelation 21:14 And the wall of the city had twelve foundations, and in them the **names of the twelve Emissaries** of the Lamb.

The book of Revelation is witness that no 13th apostle is mentioned and to the detriment of the liar Paul his name is no where to be seen in the walls of the city. Surprised? You should be and asking yourself the question why did it not mention thirteen apostles opposed to twelve? This is another testimony that Paul was a false apostle not only self proclaimed but self deceived deceiving others.

In Acts 26:16 Paul was summoned by the "bright light" of Satan and not the Rebbe Yeshua who has never appeared as a "bright light" to any of his disciples and having no physical

47

form. The bidding that Paul was doing for the bright light in which he was removing people from the Torah of YHWH, only Satan has a stake in that and no one else. Paul was doing the bidding of Satan.

> **Acts 26:16** *But rise, and stand upon your feet: for I have appeared to you for this purpose, to make you a servant and a witness both of these things which you have seen, and of those things in which I will appear to you;*

He was lying that he was called by rebbe Yeshua supernaturally to go to the gentiles. If he was called by rebbe Yeshua then why does the book of Revelation not mention thirteen apostles opposed to the original twelve? Many are blinded by foolish Pauline theologies erected by Rome. I know a lady who lives in Germany from the House of Yahudah who was given visions. In one vision in 2004 in which she was with Pope John Paul in the Vatican.

She asked him why did you not give the true law/Torah of G-d to the people. She said to him I am a Yahudit, I receive visions and I am from the tribe of Y'sra'el. He said have you not read the Catholic book. She asked him which Catholic book. He said the letter of Paul and he took her to the letter of Romans.

She said to him there is no Catholic book we only have the words of YHWH in his Torah. He quoted Romans 5 to negate the Torah. She quoted Hebrews chapter 4 about the Sabbath not been finished as part of the law.

Then he quoted Romans 7 trying to negate the Torah.

The pope said to her in the vision that Paul did not finish the book of Romans. He said Paul only finished half and we finished the other half. (As I have taught the letters of Paul have been tampered with in fact every book of the New Testament was in some way tampered and none of it can be trusted)

> **Acts 21:21** And they are informed of you, that you teach all the Yahudim which are among the Gentiles

to forsake Musa' (Moses) Torah, saying that they should not circumcise their children, neither to walk after the Halaka.

The charge brought against Paul was true because he even lied to the council that he does not teach such things when clearly his letters which were not in the hands of the council reveal otherwise. The two clear charges brought were 1, he is teaching people to forsake Moses i.e. not obey the commandments of the Torah. This charge was true as we have seen.

The second charge was that they should not circumcise the children. Once again a Torah violation, both of these charges could not be denied in light of what we have seen in his letters such as Galatians 5:2. Therefore anyone who thinks Paul was telling the truth needs to reconsider based on the faulty contradictory teachings of Paul.

One may say why would G-d do this and allow such a man to continue. The answer is simply because G-d wants to test Y'sra'el and her faithfulness.

> **Debarim (Deut) 13:1-3** If there arise among you a prophet, or a dreamer of dreams, and gives you a sign or a miracle comes to pass, 2 And the sign or the miracle that came to pass, about which he spoke to you, saying, Let us go after other powers, which You have not known, and let us serve them; 3 You shall not listen to the words of that prophet, or that dreamer of dreams: for **YHWH Your POWER is testing you**, to know whether you love YHWH Your POWER with all your heart and with all your soul.

So Paul claims he is not lying yet he lies. Remember what I told you about the Pope and Rome above.

> **Rom 9:1** I say the truth in Messiah, I lie not, my conscience also bearing me witness in the Ruakh Ha Kadosh (Set-Apart Spirit),

49

Gal 1:20 Now the things which I write to you, behold, before YHWH, I lie not.

Why does Paul have a need to say this over and over again that "he lies not"? The scroll of Deuteronomy is clear if anyone claims to be a prophet, a miracle worker and does things, says things that come to pass and then he leads people to another G-d, you are not to trust him.

Debarim (Deut) 13:5 And that prophet, or **that dreamer of dreams, shall be put to death**; because he has spoken to turn you away from YHWH Your POWER, who brought you out of the land of Mitzrayim (Egypt), and redeemed you out of the Beyth (house) of slavery, to draw you out of the way which Halaka YHWH Your POWER commanded that you keep. So shall You put the evil away from among you.

We are also told in Debarim (Deut) that we are not to be afraid of such people and they are to be put to death. If we had a Sanhedrin they would decide against Paul and put him to death for his wayward teachings of the Torah. So how do we put him to death today?

We simply refuse to walk in his statements and remove him, expunge him from our thoughts and our life; we must <u>never</u> take anything from his letters to make dogma out of. This way we have put him to death. We should not listen to anything contradictory to the Torah that he is teaching. One such teaching is Gal 5:2 that we should not circumcise.

If you are an Y'sra'elite, or even a gentile who has joined Y'sra'el you must circumcise, if you are a gentile and you have children, who are male they too must be circumcised, there is no excuse not to hold the contract of circumcision, which is everlasting.

If you do not and fall in the trap of thinking gentiles don't have to do it or there are others out there teaching you not to do it then you have violated the Torah which commands it.

Acts 21:21 And they are informed of you, that you teach all the Yahudim which are among the Gentiles to forsake Musa' (Moses) Torah, saying that they should not circumcise their children, neither to walk after the Halaka.

This is clear proof that Paul was caught teaching his false doctrines which were contrary to the Torah.

Beresheeth (Gen) 17:19 Then G-d said, No, Sarah your wife shall bear you a son, and you shall call his name Yts'hak: **I will establish My Contract, Agreement with him for an everlasting Contract**/Agreement, and with his descendants after him. **27** And all the men of his Beyth (house), **born in the Beyth (house), or bought with money** from a foreigner, were circumcised with him.

Everybody working for and living in Abraham's household was circumcised. These were predominantly gentile servants with some who had converted to the G-d of Abraham. Note they were living in Abraham's territory and not in his house literally but the Torah speaks as "the men of his beyth" which means "living in Abraham's" borders of his land that belonged to Abraham. Abraham had more than one household both in Hebron and Beersheba.

How do you think they would have reacted if they had read Paul's letters? They would have rejected him as a false prophet pure and simple and would have followed their master Abraham's voice instead. So why is it that if these foreigners can follow Abraham's voice that you have to follow Paul's voice? I take it your Master's voice is not enough that said in John 14:15 to obey the Torah and to do the Commands there in.

John 14:15 If you love me, guard and do my commandments.

51

Circumcision for men was one of these "Guard and Do" commandments. So if someone says did rebbe Yeshua command circumcision of males then the answer is YES.

It would be much more better that you follow your rebbe's voice and get circumcised than to be left uncircumcised like the gentiles running around claiming salvation but refusing to obey Abbah YHWH.

Let me tell you something of interest for those who want to know. Noakh and his son Shem were both born circumcised. Shem is our forefather through whom we the Hebrews descend. Shem literally in the Hebrew means "Name". One of the titles of G-d is 'Ha'Shem' which means (The Name).

Shem is spelt in the Hebrew with a Shin and Mem שם.

In the ancient Hebrew it means "Crown upon a people" so the Hebrew people or the "Children of Y'sra'el" were going to be taken from the people and be the crowned jewels so to speak to become YHWH's chosen seed.

Chapter 5
Paul and his band of men

We hear about different people that were either aligned with the Paul heresy or at least thought he was an Y'sra'elite believer while he was teaching some very wrong doctrines.

Yes Paul was an Y'sra'elite (Rom 11:1) but he only served the Greek agenda and the agenda of Rome to remove and negate the Torah from the people.

> **Acts 15: 1** And certain men which came down from Yahudah taught the brothers, and said, Except you be circumcised according to the custom of Musa, you cannot be rescued. 2 When therefore Paul and Bar'nabah had no small dissension and disputation with them, they determined that Paul and Bar'nabah, and certain other of them, should go up to Yerushalim to the Emissaries and elders about this question.

As can be seen Paul not just had a disagreement with the men who came down from Yahudah but also with Bar'nabah.

> **Acts 15:37-39** And Bar'nabah determined to take with them Yahukhannan (John), whose surname was Mark. 38 But Paul insisted not to take with them this one because he departed from them in Pamphylia, and had not gone with them in the work. 39 And the contention was so sharp between them, that they parted company one from the other: and so Bar'nabah took Mark, and sailed to Cyprus;

The contention was so sharp that they parted their ways eventually as Bar'nabah knew he could no longer work with Pauline ideologies which were contradictory.

His agenda did not succeed in that time as many of the Jews were quite clued up what was going on and outright rejected him.

> **Acts 20:3** And there abode three months. And when

53

the Yahudim plotted against him, as he was about to sail into Syria, he purposed to return through Makedonia (Macedonia).

One has to ask the question why would the Jews plot against him since Paul was also a Jew and if he was teaching the Torah there was no reason for the plots unless some people had a personal vendetta against him. We do not find a case of a personal vendetta either as he was not related closely with the people on a personal level neither had any business dealings with them. The only thing that he was being judged on was by what he taught. That in itself tells a lot about a man and his understanding of the sacred scrolls.

It appears that his Torah teachings were not in line with what was held to be true and believed by the Jews in the synagogue hence why various Jews did not like him and it was not as people think because of rebbe Yeshua's claim of Messiah.

The contention was not who is rebbe Yeshua but more specific to Torah and its application as we shall see in the next verse.

> **Acts 22: 21-23** And he said to me, Depart: **for I will send you far hence to the Gentiles**. 22 The crowd was listening until he said this, and then the crowd shouted, **Away with such a fellow from the earth**: for it is not fit that he should live. 23 And as they shouted, and cast off their cloaks, and threw dust into the air,

Notice what he stated

That Paul was told that "**for I will send you far hence to the Gentiles**."

This is a problem. To ordinary folks this may not mean much but to seasoned Jews who understand the Tanak that no such commandment or prophecy was given that a person, an apostle or a prophet would be chosen to send to the gentiles. This is because the "gentiles" have no contract with the G-d of Y'sra'el. If you think there is prove me wrong.

54

Rescue/Salvation is only ever given to one people and that is to the Y'sra'elites.

> **Amos 3:1-2** Hear this word that **YHWH has spoken against you, O children of Y'sra'el**, against the whole family which I brought up from the land of Mitzrayim (Egypt), saying, **2 <u>You only have I known</u>** of all the families of the earth: therefore I will punish you for all your iniquities.

So who does the G-d of Y'sra'el describe?

Not Gentiles but only the "Children of Y'sra'el". He even says YOU only have I known.

G-d is not denying that he did not create gentiles but he is making a precedent that the Contracts and promises belong to only one people called the **Children of Y'sra'el**. So when Paul goes branding the lie that he is sent to the "gentiles" this is understood as why is he going to the cats and dogs. Yes you read that correct the gentiles behave at most times in their unclean ways as cats and dogs and scripture refers to them as "dogs".

> **Exodus 11:7** But against none of the children of Y'sra'el shall a dog move its tongue,9 against man, or beast: that you may know that YHWH does make a difference between the Mitzrim (Egyptians) and Y'sra'el.

> **Psalm 22:20** Rescue my soul from the sword; my beloved life from the power of the dog.

> **Mattityahu 15:26** But he answered and said, it is not right to take the children's Lakhem (bread), and to cast it to dogs.

---

[9] Children of Y'sra'el are always special in YHWH's eyes because of our contracts established with YHWH through our forefathers. It is not because we do everything right; but the promises, and agreements, YHWH has made with our forefathers, stand forever.

As you can see all three references point to dogs as "gentiles" unless you believe that the Egyptians, Romans and the Phoenicians are the chosen people.

While Paul's agenda appears to have succeeded in a large part today to some extent in that many people of the world today are not clued up on what was the government of YHWH and how did the people obey the Torah and function on a day to day level so this is how the deception prevails. While those who have the true Ruakh of G-d (Holy Spirit) will not be deceived by such statements of Paul, others with the lack of understanding will do so and have already fallen in the pit hole. The only way to come out of that pit is by repentance and realigning yourself with the Torah, if you don't then you dig yourself in more deeper.

So there you have it, the G-d that we serve has no contract with the gentiles and to believe in such would be quite erroneous.

You may ask but what about the statement in Matthew 28:19 did not rebbe Yeshua tell the disciples to go to the "gentiles"?

Let's look at that.

> **Mat 28:19-20 (KJV)** Go ye therefore, and teach all nations, baptizing them in the name of the Father, and of the Son, and of the Holy Ghost: 20 Teaching them to observe all things whatsoever I have commanded you: and, lo, I am with you always, even unto the end of the world. Amen.

The KJV reading is shown above but look at the actual Hebrew from which the following is extracted.

> **Hidden-Truths Hebraic Scrolls Study Scriptures**
> **Matthew 28:19-20** Go to them
> **20** And teaching them to **Guard and Do** all the words of the Commandments as a witness forever.

56

Notice that in the actual favoured reading has no mention of a gentile nation but actually you are commanded to teach Torah to the people in matter of fact lost Y'sra'elites. So one can understand why suddenly the Jews became angry with Paul because they saw in him something that had not been given and his false theology was caught on by them and they were really angry. They were expecting a leader figure to rescue them Isa 2:3, but what Paul gave them was a contradictory account of himself being chosen to go seek the gentiles. This was a contradictory statement made by one who called himself from the tribe of Benyamin and an Y'sra'elite. Y'sra'elites were NEVER commanded to seek after the gentiles.

> **Acts 21:21** And they are informed of you, that you teach all the Yahudim which are among the Gentiles to forsake Musa' (Moses) Torah, saying that they should not circumcise their children, neither to walk after the Halaka.

When Paul was brought before the elders, a serious charge was brought against him that he was breaking Halacha of teaching people that they do not have to keep the Torah now, and that they do not yet have to be circumcised so this was an issue that many had with Paul and so the elders in Jerusalem had to deal with this to remove any issue of Torah violation.

Although Paul gave his excuses in Jerusalem to convince the elders otherwise, but they made him demonstrate to the people that he had still regards for the Torah and was willing to guard and obey it. However Paul had his own agenda and so conveniently escaped the wrath of the Yahudim who hated him at that time and wanted to remove him from any position of teaching.

> **Acts 21:23-24** Do therefore this that we say to you: We have four men which have a Nazarite vow on them; 24 Take them, and purify yourself with them, and pay their expenses that they may shave their heads: and all may know that those things, that they were informed concerning you, are not so; but that

57

you yourself also keep the Halaka (commandments), and obey all the Torah.

As you can see an act of demonstration of his faithfulness to the Torah was required, which he did but later he goes back to Asia Minor and teaches the same anti-Torah statements that we find in the letter of Romans, in Corinth and in Galatia etc.

> **Galatians 5:2** Behold, I Paul say to ye, that if **you be circumcised, Messiah shall profit ye nothing**.

Pastors usually take this out of context by denying the Torah of Moses and telling people that you do not have to be circumcised. Paul did confuse many people by calling circumcision <u>fleshly</u> while it was part of the Abrahamic Contract and was everlasting and this was one of the reasons Paul was summoned into the Jerusalem council.

This is one of his heretical teachings. Christians who have taken these teachings have gone into destruction by following this type of lie while G-d admonishes us to make sure we follow all His Contracts.

This letter of Galatians demonstrates to us if written by Paul that he was a wolf who is described in the prophecy in Genesis 49.

> **Genesis 49:27** Benyamin is a <u>ravenous wolf</u>: in the morning he shall devour the prey, and at night he shall divide the spoil.

Paul is not called a "wolf" for no reason. This is his description for one of the roles a Benjamite would do in the future. He will "divide" and spoil "literally" and allegorically both apply.

Chapter 6
How to recognise a false prophet or an alleged teacher

Gilyahna (Rev) 2:2 I know your works, and your labour, and your patience, and how you cannot **tolerate them which are evil**: and you have **tried them which said they are apostles, and are not and have found them liars**:

Some people consider Paul to be the false Apostle in Christianity known as "Paul the little" who they believe was teaching false doctrines or teaching against obeying the Torah which caused these people to reject Paul as a false apostle. Actually they are not wrong to make this conclusion and had good reason to do so as I explained in this book earlier.

Note most churches may be shocked to learn Paul being an Y'sra'elite of the stock of Benjamin was a man who looked like an ancient Egyptian which means a man of dark colour. How would the churches feel or the Caucasian Supremacist that the very person they use to disobey G-d is in fact Black as were the original tribes of Y'sra'el?

The scroll of Revelation's false apostles is not just about Paul but other false apostles as well that came in our history, time and space. Paul was chosen by self there was no mission for him.

We shall soon uncover who the other false apostles of Revelation are alongside Paul and where they can be found today.

There are two criteria given here by rebbe Yeshua that classified false apostles in the scroll. He said that the believing community could not tolerate their _evil._ This is the first criteria in other words anti-Torah. The second criteria was that they teach _lies_. Let's look at the first criteria.

Evil – We are going to look at two Hebrew words that fit the context, one is evil (Rayim) and the other wicked (rashayim). Both lead to each other and are very easy to differentiate.

59

The scroll of Revelation (Apocalypse) was originally written in Hebrew hence our focus is on the language and the people of that culture and not on modern or ancient gentile Greek perceptions.

In the ancient Hebrew society it was very easy to define who is evil or wicked as both were synonymous terms. You cannot be evil without equally being wicked though there may be degrees of wickedness, while evil was a general category. These days in the perverted cultures where we live wickedness or the word wicked is just seen as a slang term and a fashionable term which is not really applied to evilness in a person.

Wickedness in ancient Y'sra'el was defined as anyone who did not guard and keep the 7th day Sabbath, which was seen as evil since they did not believe in G-d or guarding His commandments i.e., the Torah. This is why gentiles were singled out and not liked as they were seen to be idolaters.

So the first way to tell if someone was evil according to the proper ancient understanding was to see if they obeyed the Sabbath law regarding the Torah.

This category was applied to people who refused to keep the Sabbath and they were separated from the assemblies and were not welcome in the assembly even being excommunicated. In ancient times the Sabbath breaking carried a capital penalty of death and it carried an excommunication order for 30 days or longer if the person refused to comply even ostracising from the community of the faithful.

This does not refer to new people such as gentiles who were coming into the faith and learning how to keep the Sabbaths. The category strictly applied to anyone within or outside Y'sra'el and stuck deep into the psyche of the people. In ancient times dinner time talk was about so and so not keeping the laws of YHWH, them being wicked and their actions being unclean. No one talked about how good the Simpson's was today. Why they use perverse language in films as it happens today is more fashion. This perverseness would be the talk of the town in ancient Y'sra'el. If we apply the same ancient criteria today then immediately you can see that many Churches fall into the category of wickedness. Not keeping the Sabbath alone will mean capital punishment of death. Most if not all of these churches are into Pauline epistles that are not scripture and thus lawless. If these buildings existed in ancient Y'sra'el no one from the Yahudim would want to sit with the Christians and eat as they would be seen to be gentiles in idolatry.

Most people think wickedness is about doing a particular crime but in essence breaking the Sabbath was/is a Torah crime and that is how this term has to be seen even today. We cannot say someone is wicked because they have four wives, a guilt often imputed on Muslims but the Torah allows polygamy and this is how the Muslims learned it. Or you cannot say someone was wicked because they swore at someone or did not attend Church.

Also one cannot say someone is wicked because they have a $100,000 Mercedes. The crime must fit the Torah and the Torah must fit the crime.

The next word to look at it is to look at the term evil.

Evil can be ranged into different degrees e.g. a man or woman slandering someone is considered evil because three persons are affected and this is considered a grave sin; a person breaking an oath was seen as evil. A person murdering another was seen as evil. A person not paying his tithe was seen as evil. Note today those who do not pay tithe are not seen as evil as there is no law established against it at least in Churches or even assemblies. However in Muslim countries if you have your money in a bank the bank automatically deducts you yearly Zakat (obligation money according to the Muslim Qur'an) and no one can challenge that decision.

A man or woman who may use unequal weights such as a shop owner or some sort of sales person who did not use the proper scales and deliberately sold goods which were

61

underweight, or of bad quality would also be considered evil but the punishment of these different types of evils is different according to the severity of the crime. Christendom thinks all sins are equal but they are not.

The second category rebbe Yeshua defined to designate evil apostles is that they teach lies. The reference to lies implies by definition a category of using the Torah to identify the lies; this is also referred to as destroying the Torah. All Christendom has done for two thousand years is destroy the Torah. Therefore they fit the category of evil.

We are talking lies here about Scripture because this is directed at an assembly and not at the common man in the street. We are not talking worldly lies such as someone stole my wallet but lies which apostles and prophets can teach if they are accused of telling lies then they are called liars for teaching lies against the kingdom. This means they are not telling you the truth about G-d and His ways. Or they may say 'The Lord has said this to me, I have received such and such word, etc, but he/she did not receive anything so that is another form of lying."

How do we weigh up lies? We examine if what has been taught lines up with Torah or not. No, we do not go looking at Paul and see if he said it or not said it; this is what Pauline Christianity does. We are least interested in that, our interest is in the laws already established in the Torah which are the 613 commandments both positive and negative. Are the lies being taught fit Torah violations? One such lie is that the food laws of Leviticus 11 do not apply to us. A similar Torah violation is we do not have to wear the head covering that is for both male and females.

A third Torah violation is we do not have to keep the seven annual feasts.

One need not go very far or even enter a church. Just sit on your sofa and switch on your remote controlled TV and change to any mainstream Christian Channel and hear how many so called alleged apostles of light, bright Pastors and

62

allegedly clever Bishops, men who call themselves prophets but do not even know the sacred name of G-d disparaging the laws of YHWH.

Teaching that the Torah is abrogated and done away with while they <u>falsely</u> claim that they know Yahushua and that He gives them grace and they are saved. This is indeed a Torah crime and a lie that the Torah itself by which everything is judged is removed out of the way which means we no longer have a mechanism to measure and punish sin. They are essentially destroying the Torah the punishment for which is death.

We do not need to hear fluffy words like "I have grace" from Christendom to be deceived and feel good about abandoning the Sabbath or other said laws. Grace was and still is available to Torah keeping people. Anyone who makes such a claim that because of rebbe Yeshua, the Torah is taken out of the way is classed as a <u>liar</u> and a Torah violator. It does not matter who he/she is. You are even warned not to welcome such people in our home (Matt 10:14). Note most of these people will use the Pauline letters because he is their ringleader hence he is one of the people named in Rev 2:2 and the city where his false theology was rejected by Ephesus and the rest of Asia Minor.

Rebbe Yeshua congratulates Ephesians for rejecting Pauline lawlessness.

> **Rev 2:2** I know your works, and your labour, and your patience, and how you cannot tolerate them which are evil: and you have tried them which said they are Emissaries, and are not, and have found them liars:

In Second Timothy 1:15 Paul confirms this.

> **Second Timothy 1:15** This you know, that all they which are in Asia Minor (Turkey) deserted me; of whom are Phygellus and Hermogenes.

These are the kind of people the scroll of Revelation speaks about. They both lie and are evil. Anyone who has used or still

63

uses a mere man such as Paul in the context of teaching that you can <u>now</u> break the law of our great El YHWH because Paul said so is by definition evil, wicked and a liar. We are not talking about local council legislation of a city or civil laws in a locality here but the laws made by the lawmaker of the Universe. Are we to believe that one individual like Paul of Tarsus who can waltz along and annul all laws? Bravo, this is what a Christendom is teaching today. How foolish!

How dare anyone do this trying to destroy the Torah? This is the ridiculous foolish teachings of Christendom, which has been representing for nearly 1900 years. For your information Christianity was not started by rebbe Yeshua and His disciples. Yahushua stayed within Judaism and functioned in Judaism but Christianity was started by the likes of Paul of Tarsus in his own little sect. Yeshua is not G-d nor G-d come man, nor the Messiah. He did not fulfil any of the Tanak prophesies that ware specifically for the King Messiah.

Theubuthis another corrupt bishop, Marcion and Ignatius, the co called saints are the early chief propagators of the Torah has become abrogated lie. These are also Suns-day worshippers, which is forbidden in the Torah. Later, Ezekiel the prophet spoke out against people worshipping the deity of the sun on the suns-day in Ezekiel chapter 8:12-16.

> **Y'khezki'el (Ezek) 8:11-16** And there stood before them seventy men of the elders of the house of Y'sra'el, and in the midst of them stood Yaazanyahu (Jaazaniah) the son of Shaphan, with every man his censer in his hand; and a thick cloud of incense went up. **12** Then said he to me, Son of man, have you seen what the elders of the house of Y'sra'el do in the dark, every man in the chambers of his imagery? For they say, YHWH sees us not; YHWH has forsaken the earth. **13** He said also to me, Turn yet again, and you shall see greater abominations that they do. **14** Then he brought me to the door of the gate of YHWH's house which was toward the north; and, behold, there sat

women weeping[10] for Tammuz.[11] **15** Then said he to me, Have you seen this, O son of man? Return yet again, and you shall see greater abominations than these. **16** And he brought me into the inner court of YHWH's house, and, behold, at the door of the Temple of YHWH, between the porch and the altar, were about twenty-five men, with their backs toward the Temple of YHWH, and their faces toward the east; and they petitioned the sun toward the east.

These people and others such as Justin Martyr, Constantine and the various Popes that took over from them. The evidence for Justin Martyr of believing the Torah was given as a punishment to Y'sra'el can be seen in his debate with Trypho the Jew and to teach that it is now no longer required. Justin Martyr was a Greek surprise, surprise. Was it not Antiochus Epiphanes the Greek who also tried to destroy the Torah!

Justin speaks chapter 10 of his dialog with Trypho:

> "My friends, is there any other accusation you have against us than this, that we [Justin and co] do not observe the Law [Torah], nor circumcise the flesh as your forefathers did, nor keep the sabbaths as you do? Or do you also condemn our customs and morals?

These words can be read of Justin who admits they the Christians do not obey the Torah/LAW, they do not circumcise and they do not keep or safe guard the Sabbath.

---

[10] These were Temple prostitutes crying during the 40 days fast declared by Semaramis for death of her son Tammuz.

[11] http://www.pantheon.org/articles/t/tammuz.html
The Akkadian vegetation-god, counterpart of the Sumerian Damuzi and the symbol of death and rebirth in nature. He is the son of Ea and husband of Ishtar. Each year he dies in the hot summer (in the month tammus, June/July) and his soul is taken by the Gallu demons to the underworld. Woe and desolation fall upon the earth, and Ishtar leads the world in lamentation. She then descends to the nether world, ruled by Ereshkigal, and after many trials succeeds in bringing him back, as a result of which fertility and joy return to the earth. In Syria he was identified with Adonis.

Trypho addresses Justin:

[2] "This last charge is what surprises us," replied Trypho. "Those other charges which the rabble lodge against you are not worthy of belief, for they are too repulsive to human nature. But the precepts in what you call your Gospel are so marvelous and great that I don't think that anyone could possibly keep them. For I took the trouble to read them. [3] But this is what surprises us most, that you who claim to be pious and believe yourselves to be different from the others do not segregate yourselves from them, nor do you observe a manner of life different from that of the Gentiles, for you do not keep the feasts or sabbaths, nor do you practice the rite of circumcision. You place your hope in a crucified man, and still expect to receive favors from G-d when you disregard His commandments. Have you not read that the male who is not circumcised on the eighth day will be cut off from his people? [Gen 17.14] This precept was for stranger and purchased slave alike. [4] But you, forthwith, scorn this covenant, spurn the commands that come afterwards, and then you try to convince us that you know G-d, when you fail to do those things that every G-d-fearing person would do. If, therefore, you can give a satisfactory reply to these charges and can show us on what you place your hopes, even though you refuse to observe the Law, we will listen to you most willingly, and then we can go on and examine in the same manner our other differences."

Justin speaks against the Law;

Chapter 11

"Trypho," I began, "there never will be, nor has there ever been from eternity, any other G-d except Him who created and formed this universe. Furthermore, we do not claim that our G-d is different from yours, for He is the G-d who, with a strong hand and outstretched arm, led your forefathers out of the land of Egypt. Nor have we placed our trust in any other (for, indeed, there is no other), but only in Him whom you also have trusted,

66

the G-d of Abraham and of Isaac and of Jacob. But, our hope is not through Moses or through the Law, otherwise our customs would be the same as yours. [2] Now, indeed, for I have read, Trypho, that there should be a definitive law and a covenant, more binding than all others, which now must be respected by all those who aspire to the heritage of G-d. **The law promulgated at Horeb is already obsolete, and was intended for you Jews only**, whereas the law of which I speak is simply for all men. Now, a later law in opposition to an older law abrogates the older; so, too, does a later covenant void an earlier one. An everlasting and final law, Christ Himself, and a trustworthy covenant has been given to us, after which there will be no law, or commandment, or precept.

First of all Justin is contradicting himself just like his teacher Paul of Tarsus by saying that the G-d that he serves is the same as the Christian G-d. Really! That is news to me. Then why do the Christians not obey the law/Torah? Since Justin admitted as the Christians do that they serve the same G-d.

Justin the Greek admitted that he does not regard the contracts and called the ancient contracts in the Torah that are permanently binding annulled over a renewed contract. This could not be further from the truth because no contract is ever annulled!

All contracts/covenants run parallel with each other with different principle values, just as on an airport all airplanes fly to different destinations. Does the flight from London to New York cancel the flight from London to Paris and make it obsolete? No! The fallacy of Christendom and the likes of Justin is to believe that one contract cancels another which reveals Justin and his forbears know little to nothing about our Torah contracts/agreements.

Each Torah contract is mutually exclusive and may have parallel commands yet different application such as the contract given to Abraham in Gen 17:4 in regards to fleshly circumcision, while the contract that G-d made with Noakh in Gen 9:11 was a contract/agreement not to destroy the earth ever again. As demonstrated by this Lewite/Kohen, it can be seen that both contracts given at different times are mutually

67

exclusive and parallel yet both are in force today. Can anyone deny that?

So if you have stopped going to a lying church, good for you and unless you are going to teach them Torah best stay clear of their false teachings and vain glory. This is why Christianity has lost its appeal to many people for its lies and vain glory. You turn to any Christian TV channel and it's the same bad teachings they teach, which is grace but the law of YHWH is set aside and ignored. Imagine what sort of chaos we would have in our institutions if we did the same thing for secular law?

It's so foolish like driving a car without tyres. Flying without engines on a plane but the ignorant and the uneducated have believed these lies and have been deceived. These are the teachings that you have believed out of the pit of She'ol whose author is not the Most High but Satan.

Ask them where is the law of G-d? Who nailed it to the pagan cross? How dare they teach such blatant lies that a pagan cross can take away the laws of G-d and be set aside?

If they reject Torah then they cannot have anything, no law equals lawlessness and no grace. The local law states that you shall not cause disorder or break property. If you then go and break someone's property and the policeman arrives to arrest you, he does not pat you on the back, but arrests you. What do you tell him? The local laws are nailed to the cross and I have grace to break the property? You can see the disbelieving look on the policeman's face when he slams the hand cuffs on you and throws you in the back of his car to take you to police station to lock you up.

Here is a classical verse that the Christians use to break YHWH's holy law.

> **1Co 9:20 (KJV)** And unto the Jews I became as a Jew, that I might gain the Jews; to them that are under the law, as under the law, that I might gain them that are under the law;

68

First Cor 9:20 (HTHS) And to the Yahudim I became as a Yahudi, that I might gain the Yahudim; to them that are under the human government, as under the human government, that I might gain them that are under this human law;

Here is a true translation of what is being said but was perverted by Christendom which squarely puts them and their clergy into the category of wickedness and evil.

So here Paul himself claims he became a Yahudi to the Yahudim (Jew to the Jews), I became a Yahudi and to those who being 'under the law' meaning that these people are in bondage under men's idea of salvation and not YHWH's he became like them. This is not speaking about Torah but **HUMAN GOVERNMENT** or **RABBINIC LAW**. It is certain that all of us before realizing hard truths thought if I am a good person then surely I will go to heaven. This is common thinking in the gentiles. However, first, heaven is coming down to us and second who defines "Good?" Your president, the Prime Minister, the law legislators, or is "Good" defined by the Most High YHWH? Did the rebbe Yeshua teach to become like gentiles? No. Paul clearly contradicts the words of his rebbe.

Two thousand years ago a similar confused rich man specifically came to rebbe Yeshua and you know rich men are usually confused with their wealth and how to use it wisely however they know how to make wealth. They have the idea that if they give money to the poor, build an odd hospital, put up a school and give money to the politicians, who will help them in their businesses. They attend a few dinners for charities and then continue to do all the worldly evils that they are accustomed to, their belief is that this will exempt them from hell and the Creator will look the other way for them and allow them entry. This is their way of appeasing the G-d.

However this rich man in Y'sra'el who went to the rebbe Yeshua did not go to the Sanhedrin. He did not go to the Roman rulers in charge. He did not even go to the ruler of the Torah teachers in the Temple. That was Nicodemus a right-

69

ruling man and he went straight to the young Rabbi who had just appeared on the scene, visibly carrying no wealth, no cheer leaders surrounded him, no drummers singing his praises but only his expression of love. His compassion became his hallmark (mercy and truth). His reputation as a man of the people proceeded before him, which had spread like wild fire. People came from all over Y'sra'el to see and just to touch this man even to touch his tzitzits on his clothes was an honour for some which had the power for healing people (Matt 9:20). They wanted to know this man was real, even the Roman men in authority searched for him to help them.

The men of Galil were known as superb teachers of the Torah and extremely knowledgeable in Halacha. This is something that bothered the Temple authorities and created some tensions between them so they joked about the Galilean accent being inferior as might the English today say about the Scottish or Irish accent. This new rebbe Yeshua was not just charismatic but did extraordinary miracles he was not just a teacher but a teacher with some extra abilities with powers to silence the demons. In a debate He could defeat the best teacher in the country in a short thrift sentence. Imagine having him as your teacher then what would you become?

It may have been a privilege for some men to become his students. What is not known by many that often times Rabbis chose their students (John 15:18).

This rich man in Y'sra'el came to Him knowing that the rebbe would pull no punches and would not hold back truth hence he asked Him boldly.

Let's read what Matthew the Lewite his relative tells us.

> **Mattityahu 19:16-18** And, behold, one came and said to him, Rebbe, what Good mitzvoth (deeds) shall I do, that I may have eternal life? **17** And he said to him, Why ask me concerning the good? There is indeed one good, if you want to enter into Life, ***GUARD AND DO THE COMMANDMENTS***. **18** He said to him which

70

ones? Yahushua said, you shall do no murder, You shall not commit adultery, You shall not steal, You shall not bear false witness,

This human law holds people in bondage as it does even to this day so nothing has changed in over 2000 years. In our society where one is taught if you are a good man you can live and when you die you will go to heaven. We have now come to realize such things are simply not true because salvation came through the Contracts established by the Abbah YHWH. Those who keep claiming the blood but reject the Torah are deceived by the Church clergy and the Christian TV and Radio Stations are playing the part in spreading the devil's work and lack understanding.

Many years ago G-d told me to go back to Moses where I could find the Truth so I looked at Moses, his movie the Ten Commandments. G-d told me to follow him so I did, stepping into the Torah. My exile brought me one step closer to the G-d of my forefathers in order to obey the Torah and finish my exile eventually to go home to the land of my forefathers.

Many of my people are still in exile in Africa, Haiti, Cuba, India, Pakistan, Mauritius and other Eastern lands. They are also in Europe and other Western nations such as America, Canada and Australia where they were taken as slaves including Latin America.

Many of these still need to know who they are. They have adopted the religions of their slave masters like Christendom and Islam. Both of these religions enslaved my people and have kept them in idolatry to this day. They need to look back at the prophecy of Moses who said this would happen.

> **Deut 28:36** YHWH shall bring you, and your Sovereign which You shall set over you, to a heathen nation which neither You nor Your ahvot (fathers) have known; and there shall You serve other powers [G-ds], of **wood and stone**.

71

When I was restored to my G-d and I read the bible for the first time I cried. I pleaded why you waited until I was thirty-five years old? Why did you not call me in my youth that I may serve you? Yet today many of you happily serve wood (pagan cross) and stone (Allah) in the Ka'aba in Mecca, Saudi Arabia. I argued with my wife to tell her the truth but she rejected my message. I fought with my family but they rejected my message. I said to G-d that now you have revealed yourself to me what about all the problems I am facing with. It is too much for me. How will I face my family? How will I live with the family who rejects my message? What will happen to me? I would sit in my car and cry on my own I would go to the bathroom and cry, hiding away from my wife and children I would cry in my bedroom. I would hide in the spare guest room and cry with the bible in my hands. It was during one of these times that I went into my car that G-d gave me the following scripture.

> **Jer 29:11** For I know the plans that I have for you, says YHWH, plans of a future of shalom (peace) and prosperity and not of evil, to give you an expected reward.

I said to him right now everything is upside down. Why did you call me? Why did you not show yourself to my family? I knew this message for me was fundamentally very important and for others who will hear it but it was not for my family. I asked him this time "What about my dying son, will you heal him since he was born with a congenital disease?" He responded "he will exalt me as he is."

This is what I was told by the Master YHWH, I am talking about. I am not talking about some wishy washy church 'Jesus' that tells you keep breaking my Torah but I still love you.

I was instructed in no uncertain terms "you are not to keep the feasts of the nations" back in 1998. Yes Christmas belongs to Christians and he called Christmas the feast of the nations. Does that sound like YHWH recognised these people as his own? No. He called them goyim or gentiles which means they are not His people unless they repent and return to the ways

72

of the Torah. Does He do miracles for them? Yes, only because he is compassionate towards the whole world and not because He has any obligations to them.

The bottom line is this that Abbah YHWH can speak to people directly or through his angels, he will not allow anyone to enter the coming kingdom who are Torah violators even if they are alive and if they are dead they will remain dead since they rejected YHWH's sacred LAW which is better than gold. It is better than silver and all the money in the banks of the world put together has no comparison to it.

> **Tehillim (Ps) 19:9-11** The fear of YHWH is clean, enduring forever: the judgments of YHWH are true and right-ruling altogether. **10 MORE TO BE DESIRED ARE THEY THAN GOLD**, yes, than much fine gold: sweeter also than honey and the honeycomb.**11** Moreover by them is your servant warned: and in keeping of them there is great reward.

If you feel that somehow you will squeeze through the door of the Kingdom even if you do not obey and keep the Torah or that you have some kind of magic formula by saying the term 'Jesus', I tell you the truth Abbah will not allow it. If he allowed such foolish things the angels will say on that Day, why did you cast us out for rebellion when sinning humans had been allowed to enter who had not obeyed nor acknowledged his set-apart sanctified law as life.

False Prophets

> **Ma'aseh Schilichim (Acts) 13:6** And when they had gone through the isle to Paphos, they found a certain sorcerer, a **false prophet,** and a Yahudi, whose name was Bar-Yeshua (Jesus).

Now there was a man called by the name of bar Jesus (Bar-Yeshua), who was a false prophet and a Yahudi. We have one by the same name masquerading in many churches today called 'Jesus' who also is the false prophet teaching lawlessness through his disciples in Churches.

The false Jesus or Borgia Cesare the mixed race, see article "Do you love Jesus or Borgia Cesare."
http://www.african-Y'sra'el.com/Simon/HTML/Do%20you%20love%20Jesus%20or%20Borgia%20Cesare.html

> **Tehillim (Ps) 101:7** He <u>that works deceit</u> shall **not dwell within my house**: he that **speaks falsehoods** shall not **stand in front of my eyes**.

If you work any kind of deceit such as saying the law is done away or proclaim falsehood, you are already doomed and you cannot stand in His presence until you repent and turn back to the Torah with obedience. Yes you may not know how to keep the commandments but this is where you are suppose to get a Rabbi with good understanding and knowledge in Torah like myself and ask. You do not continue to function by remaining in paganism and hoping for the best. The Most High is not going to punish you for unknown ignorance but He will punish for disobedience. The two are mutually exclusive. If once you know what a teacher of the Torah has told you and you do not do the necessary then you are responsible for the punishment that will come upon you.

What if the teacher of the Torah misleads you? Then he has to bear your punishment so he must know what he is teaching is in accordance with Torah. If a man who calls himself a teacher is a Kohen/Levite then these were/are the people appointed for the eternal priesthood. Many people from Judah also became teachers but they were not priests. They knew Torah and could teach it but they had to rely on minutiae details from the experts of the Torah hence the Levites. So if you have a Kohen as a teacher then consider yourself in good hands.

False prophets and their identification

Many times I am asked how to identify those around us who are true or are motivated by greed and really wolves in sheep's clothing. In today's world how do we recognise who is called by G-d and who isn't?

74

There are certain things given in scripture to help us. First and foremost anyone and it should not matter who that anyone is if he/she suggests that a revival is coming you should have your lights blinking at that moment because that person speaks from ignorance not knowing Scriptures because NO ENDTIME REVIVAL IS TO TAKE PLACE. Shocked! I thought you might be. YES THERE IS NO END TIME REVIVAL. In fact the Hebrew Scriptures speak about an END TIME hard survival for the TRUE believers. Who will survive? There is something called an End-Time Restoration that will take place and has been showing signs of picking up momentum amongst the true Hebrew Y'sra'elites, the people of colour.

We must prove everything we say by at least two witnesses IF anyone insists on these kinds of revival theologies taken out of Pauline epistles are utterly false, which are simply born out of dogmatism and presumptuousness of Christendom!

Let me give you now two independent witnesses to verify what I just said earlier because if I did not then I would equally be a false prophet and bad teacher:

First witness King Solomon

> **Second Chronicles 7:14** If my people, which are called by my name, shall humble themselves, and petition, and seek my face, and turn from their wicked ways [Torah violations]; then will I hear from shamayim, and will forgive their transgression, and will heal their land.

There is a clear inference in this scripture that at the End of Days there will be much apostasy and those that turn back to Torah will be redeemed in the kingdom to come. Rebbe Yeshua taught full Torah compliance but Rome turned him into their Messiah and G-d.

There is also an apostasy marked for the End of Days which is now being seen widely. Have you heard of the term Chris-Islam? It is happening where Christians are doing readings of the Muslim sacred book called the Qur'an. It's very widespread.

The apostasy is so large that we will see it and know it and indeed it is because large scale ministries are falling into this. It is happening right now as I speak. Have you seen it? The apostate church yes that is right the church where people are apologising to people like Darwin the atheist. Why would a Church that believed in a Creator G-d be apologising to Darwin who led so many billions astray by his false humanist theology that has no basis on the selection and creation of species?

We see such apostasy in Churches where Church folks are made to apologise to abject homosexual sinners who refuse to repent.

Today people rely on facts however these facts and truth are mutually exclusive. A fact can be derived out of some scientific research that is subject to change with time so therefore it cannot even be proven to be true but a truth always remains the truth and is unchangeable. It needs no scientific enquiry.

It's a known fact that the Europeans have accepted a Caucasian looking G-d/man in their churches but it's not the TRUTH as that is simply living in idolatry.

See the difference between facts and truths. Fact that the Ashkenazi Jews are the chosen but the truth is that the true people of the book, the chosen were/are black Negro looking people and not white people. Those Ashkenazim are converts out of Khazaria, now there is something to blow some away.

G-d always use the colour white for the plague of leprosy as a judgement. This is how the white populations of Europe were used to judge true Black Y'sra'el, who they made their slaves, look who made the black slaves; they were carried in Jewish owned and Christian run ships neither of which at the time were chosen. Yes that is a hard TRUTH and that Caucasian Jews who are not chosen but converts into Judaism, a lot of Sephardic Jews were involved in the cross Atlantic slave trade that afflicted our people the real chosen Y'sra'el. How many times do you hear this truth from your churches? How about NEVER.

The simple truth is the Church has failed true Y'sra'el and was never a true entity and never will be until G-d will one day disband and break it up. Who will recognise all the signs of the apostasy that is happening right now?

We see so much falling now because homosexuals are being ordained in the churches and have been for a while now! This is one type of falling away from truth or should I say the small truths that the Church had have now been slowly and surely discarded for this evil and wicked trend.

Paul's letters are not inspired and are leading many people into destruction. He was a false prophet as well though Peter refuted him kindly and rebbe Yeshua said there are false apostles. He was one of them but did you recognise that? You can listen to some teachings on our site illustrating this very point.

False teachers: They are inside the many established churches of today deceiving people that the Torah of Moses is done away or that it is only for the Jews. Anyone saying this fits the class of a false teacher and a false prophet and should not be given any attention yet many of you have not only given your time but haven been taken in by their doctrines such as the lie of the rapture!!!

All early believers one were Jews and up to 135 CE worshipped in the local synagogues and went to the Temple in Jerusalem before its destruction. There was no such thing as a religion called Christianity until Theoubutus, Marcion and Ignatius started their so called Christian cults alongside Rome, which are followed by many today. These types of Christians still hate the Torah as outdated.

What Truth? The Torah of the prophet Moses.

If anyone is teaching repentance but there is no description of what that repentance is, than this is suspicious. Repentance must be turning away from sin and <u>obedience</u> to the Torah, to obeying the commandments such as Sabbath, appointed times, kosher laws, circumcision and wearing tzitzits, head coverings for both men and women. The men must have beards even if its a one day beard. Is the alleged man or woman proclaiming this? If not ignore that person, it does not matter how many miracles or prophesies they have done. All these things are our tests. They must know the sacred name of G-d.

> **Deut 13:1-3** If there arise among you a prophet, or a dreamer of dreams, and gives you a sign or a miracle comes to pass, 2 And the sign or the miracle that came to pass, about which he spoke to you, saying, Let us go after other G-d, which You have not known, and let us serve them; 3 You shall not listen to the words of that prophet, or that dreamer of dreams: for YHWH your G-d is testing you, to know whether you love YHWH your G-d with all your heart and with all your soul.

It is clear if someone is leading you to repentance but back into backslidden Christianity, which is already fallen down then you stay clear of that person. It matters little how many miracles or his signs were true. He is a false prophet and not from YHWH. He must lead you to YHWH and to Torah. Anything less is not acceptable.

Paul claimed to be preaching the gospel of Christ he mentions it 10 times. What is so called concocted Pauline gospel of Christ? For references see Rom 1:16; Rom 15:9 and 29:1.

Then he mentions preaching <u>his</u> gospel Rom 2:16, 16:25, and 2 Tim 2:8. How many gospels has he got?

Rebbe Yeshua taught only one gospel, the gospel of the Kingdom that is Torah my friends, while Paul does not mention it <u>even</u> once. What a surprise is it not? See Matthew 4:23 and Mark 1:14.

Let us examine it:

78

Matthew 4:23 And Yahushua went about all over Galil, teaching in their Qahalim [Synagogues], and preaching the besorah of the kingdom, and healing all manner of sickness and all manner of disease among the people.

Rebbe Yeshua went about in synagogues preaching the Torah which is the besorah (gospel) of Kingdom (Kingdom means G-d) there is no other gospel. Just go to a synagogue today and see what they teach, it will be nothing other than this. The synagogues have Torah readings weekly and haftorah readings.

Mark 1:14 Now after that Yahukhannan (John) was put in prison, Yahushua came into Galil, preaching the besorah of G-d,

Why would rebbe Yeshua go into Galil and teach? This is because during the Roman occupation some would perhaps want to rebel and join the Romans and follow their pagan way of life so in order to preserve culture and our way of life and to show fulfilment rebbe Yeshua preached the Torah called the "Gospel of the Kingdom". There is only one kingdom and that is not some airy fairy made up one. It is the same as it was in Moses's time.

By the way Paul lied as he was given no such gospel. The gospel is Torah and anything less is a heresy. The Christian church that came up from the likes of Marcion has been teaching this heresy of abrogating Torah for 2000 years. Paul who claims the gospel as "his gospel" or "gospel of Christ/anointed" was actually never given . He was quite self cantered, in all of his letters he actually mentioned little to nothing of the real rebbe's teaching. How is it that he never once in all his epistles makes a single direct quote of rebbe Yeshua? If you don't believe me go and look at the Red Letter Bible and see how many of rebbe Yeshua's words are in the Pauline epistles. Most men are deceived in that he never met him. He met Satan as the light that deceived him. We know Satan is a bright light that can deceive people and Paul is evidence of that.

79

Ezekiel 28:17 Your heart was lifted up because of your beauty; you have corrupted your wisdom by **reason of your brightness**: I will cast you to the ground; I will lay you before Sovereigns, that they may behold you.

This is because most of his letters are tainted and corrupted by Rome to remove the Torah. He himself fell short of teaching the complete Torah teachings. This was the reason why he was summoned to the Jerusalem council in Acts 15 to answer for allegations of short changing people by teaching anti-Torah teachings.

Chapter 7
Paul's heretical cult

Docetism

Paul taught this and this was also taught by Marcion later when he cobbled up ten of Paul's letters to make up his New Testament that Christendom loves today.

In the present New Testament the gospels are ignored and Paul is exalted so he is the Christian little g-d they worship and listen to. Little do these people realise what blasphemies they commit denying and subtracting the Torah the true sacred text and idolatry calling a man G-d namely their Christ.

It does not stop here. Paul goes on to make many blasphemous statements such as G-d does not live in Temples. Acts 17:24.

Pauline claims

> **Acts 17:24** The G-d that made the world and all things therein, seeing that he is Master of the shamayim and the earth, does not dwell in temples made with hands;

Did rebbe Yeshua say otherwise; yes read below.

> **Matthew 23:21** And who shall swear by the Beyth HaMikdash (Temple), swears by it, and by **Him that dwells therein**.

> Three and a half years prior to the Temple's destruction, an Y'sra'elite Rabbi named Jonathan said that at the Mount of Olives a "bat kol a supernatural voice from heaven" issued forth, announcing, 'Return Oh backsliding children, Return unto me, and I will return unto you. [and] when they did not repent, it said, I will return to my place." (G.H. Eliason, *The Generations of Antichrist* (2010)) This voice speaking

81

continued for three and a half years prior to the destruction of the Temple. (John McClintock & James Strong, *McClintock & Strong Cyclopedia* (1877)).

This phenomena continued until the destruction of the Herodian Temple.

In other words G-d's Shekinah did not depart until just before the destruction of the Temple, now re-examine Pauline false teachings.

Tacitus a Roman historian records that when the Roman soldiers were about to enter in 70 CE into the Temple precinct, a voice spoke and said that it was now leaving:

> Contending hosts were seen meeting in the skies, arms flashed, and suddenly **the temple was illumined with fire from the clouds**. Of a sudden the doors of the shrine opened and **a superhuman voice** cried: "**The G-ds are departing**": at the same moment the mighty stir of their going was heard. 2 Few interpreted these omens as fearful; the majority firmly believed that their ancient priestly writings contained the prophecy that this was the very time when the East should grow strong and that men starting from Judea should possess the world. This mysterious prophecy had in reality pointed to Vespasian and Titus, but the common people, as is the way of human ambition, interpreted these great destinies in their own favour, and could not be turned to the truth even by adversity. 3 We have heard that the total number of the besieged of every age and both sexes was six hundred thousand: there were arms for all who could use them, and the number ready to fight was larger than could have been anticipated from the total population. Both men and women showed the same determination; and if they were to be forced to change their home, they feared life more than death.

(From Tacitus (trans. C. H. Moore) *Histories* III 4-5 and *Annals* 1-3 (Loeb Classical Library; Cambridge: Harvard University Press, 1931) at 193-9.

Pauline heresy of justified by faith
Paul claims we are justified by faith in Romans 5:1 And Ephesians 2:8. Let us examine this.

> **Eph 2:8** (KJV) For by grace are ye saved through faith; and that not of yourselves: it is the gift of G-d:

> **Romans 5:1** (KJV) Therefore being justified by faith, we have peace with G-d through our Lord Jesus Christ:

This is where the Christian "grace" heresy came from.

> **Luke 13:24** Strive to enter in at the narrow door...

Rebbe Yeshua never taught justification by faith. In fact he stated very clearly what gave eternal life through the Torah contract. To obey that <u>very</u> contract by stating the contract to obey the Torah commandments when speaking to the young man about eternal life as follows:

> **Matthew 19:17** And he said to him, Why ask me concerning the good? There is indeed one good, if you want to enter into Life, **<u>Guard and Do the commandments</u>**.

The "Guard and DO" is related to maintaining a contractual relationship with the Abbah in the heavens, we Y'sra'elites under that more than anyone what that means as we are still outside in the nations suffering for the transgressions of our forefathers. You break the contract then there is no contract left and no relationship to maintain. It's like buying a house on a loan from bank then refusing to make the loan payments on it as you signed on the dotted lines that you would make a certain payment each month for 25 years. Now if you later refuse to do that would the bank simply ignore this and continue to let you stay in the house? Or would they take court action and throw you out of the house and foreclose?

83

The same way G-d made contracts with our forefathers and if we do not <u>continue</u> in those contracts we no longer can claim any type of heretical grace as Paul claims in Eph 2:8. It's not a gift but a contract. Sorry folks you have been deceived by a grace theology as no such exists.

Does the Torah teach salvation by faith or is salvation incumbent upon fulfilling the Torah Contract?

> **Deuteronomy 6:25** And it shall be our right-ruling, if we **<u>observe to do</u>** all these commandments before YHWH our G-d, as he has commanded us.

As you can see our right-ruling is by the obedience to the Torah commandments through the contracts. If you are in the contract you are IN or else you are OUT. The crowd that brought the statement BY FAITH only in their own ignorance teach such a thing while even some of the other New Testament writers do not agree with such statements;

> **Jacob (James) 2:14** What does it profit, my Y'sraeli brethren, though a man say he has belief, and have no works? Can **belief rescue him**?

Why would Jacob (James is not his real name) make this statement if it was all about "faith"? Even Jacob understood that without demonstrating works which were required as part of the contract signed with G-d else it was impossible to claim any kind of Salvation/Rescue.

The Pauline epistles also claim we are justified by circumcision mentioned in Romans 4:11.

> **Rom 4:11 (KJV)** And he received the sign of circumcision, a **seal of the righteousness of the faith** which he had yet being uncircumcised: that he might be the father of all them that believe, though they be not circumcised; that righteousness might be imputed unto them also:

84

But also he taught assent theology which can be clearly read in Romans 4:11 and Romans 10:9.

> **Romans 10:9** That if you shall confess with your mouth Rebbe Yeshua, and shall believe in your heart that YHWH has raised him from the dead, you shall be rescued.

Can you show me in a single place in the Torah in the law of G-d where it says we can do this just by believing in our hearts?

Let me give you an example. Did Abbah YHWH threaten the people in Noakh's time with a flood by saying just believe in your heart that I am He and you shall all be rescued? Clearly not. But this is what the Churches world over teach. This is the lynchpin of Christendom. Total bunch of lies!!! How can you ever be rescued by such lies? The only place safe to be rescued by YHWH is outside the Church and not inside unless that building is teaching to Guard and Do the Torah just as rebbe Yeshua commanded in Matthew 28:19-20.

How come Paul never recognised the voice of rebbe Yeshua? Rebbe Yeshua said his sheep recognise his voice (John 10:4 and 27).

> **John 10:4, 27** (4) And when he puts forth his own sheep, he goes before them, and the sheep follow him: for they know his voice. (27) My sheep hear my voice, and I know them, and they follow me:

However Paul admitted he did not recognise his voice in Acts 9:5. You can argue all you like but you will not fix anything that he contradicts about himself.

> **Acts 9:5** And he said, who are you, Master? And the Master said, I am Yahushua whom you persecute.

Paul was nothing short of a master of contradictions. One minute he is saying something in favour of Torah and the very next minutes he is against it.

Paul was not one of the sheep. The book of Genesis tells us Paul (Benyamin) was a wolf as a future prophecy.

> **Genesis 49:27** Benyamin is a ravenous wolf: in the morning he shall devour the prey, and at night he shall divide the spoil.

Some people also have fallen in error by believing that Paul's claims of miracles in Second Corinthians 12:12 and Romans 15:9 somehow prove his apostleship while Yahushua said no to such miracles in Matthew 7:21-23 saying he would tell them "I never knew you."

> **Second Corinthians 12:12** Truly the signs of an Emissary were performed among you in all patience, in signs, and wonders, and mighty deeds.

Paul blows his own trumpet!

Here Paul's dual contradictions of Yahushua where Paul claims such miracles are proof. Paul did not know the real Yahushua and was neither commissioned as an apostle. He was an apostate self proclaimed apostle. Its more likely Rome commissioned him and most of his writings are likely authored by Rome as well.

Rebbe Yeshua taught the besorah (gospel) of the Kingdom to endure to the end.

> **Mat 10:22** (KJV) And ye shall be hated of all *men* for my name's sake: but he that endureth to the end shall be saved.

The Greek word is sozo G4982 is used in Matthew 10:22.

The Hebrew word from where the original thought came from is the word Yasha the original language of the gospels was Hebrew. Yasha means to defend, deliver, save and of course **Rescue**.

Most of the Christian world knows the rebbe as Jesus but his real Hebrew name is Yahushua, which is derived from Yasha.

Which men is Rebbe Yeshua talking about in Matthew 10:22? Well these men could be your family. When you have rejected the religion where you were brought up as false and reverted to following the Rebbe Yeshua, many people in your family will hate you. Those stuck to a man-made religion devoid of truth do not want to reason but only want to accept man-made traditions should be left to it.

In my case that was leaving Islam. That caused hatred and friction in my family and it was rocked the boat and a very big boat at that.

In some cases it may be that you were brought up as a Jehovah's witness or Mormon or perhaps even Hindus and you were brought to the realization through Ha Em Chokmah (The Holy Spirit) that you are in the wrong faith and you decide to leave this to follow the truth but you will be hated for that by your own family.

In Islam when this happens the consequences can be fatal. So the Rebbe Yeshua spoke and said in Matthew 10:21

> **Matthew 10:21** And the brother shall hand over brother to death and the Ab his child: and the children shall rise up against their parents, and cause them to be put to death.

When Muslims convert your relatives could rise up to kill you as they feel the family honour is betrayed.

A Muslim man who converted in Palestine had his body sent home in four pieces. The radical Muslims cut him down and murdered him while he was trying to give leaflets.

I have heard of Muslim parents who converted to follow the Rebbe Yeshua being put to death or others have been threatened to be put to death. One family in Pakistan, the father and the mother had to go into hiding as their sons were Muslims and threatened to kill them.

What if you are a Jehovah's Witness, Mormon or perhaps even a Hindu. Then the consequences may not be as serious as death but your family will still cut you off from fellowship or refuse to talk to you so families employ psychological punishment.

> **Matthew 10:23** But when they persecute ye in this city, flee into another: for verily I say to you, You shall not have gone over the cities of Y'sra'el, till the Son of Man returns.

The rebbe is saying to leave the city in which there is danger of death or persecution. So if a Muslim converts and his life is in danger in a particular city he must leave that city and start his life in another city with new people and even a new family. The same with a Jehovah's Witness. The Master is not telling us that we must stay to die as if there is some merit in deliberate death.

He is also saying when we go to proclaim Torah truths to the exiles of Y'sra'el we will not be able to go to all the cities where they are living.

The Ten tribes were exiled in Assyria, borders of Iran in Cities in the Mountains of the Medes. These are Kurdi areas. Can someone reach these remote parts today? It is still very difficult to make the journey to go there where we have Nestorian Christians in the cities of the Medes. These cities are very deep in the Mountains and quite difficult to reach even today. People have to travel there with mules and by walk and often times some die by falling off a cliff or into a stream.

I also want to point out that the tribes never returned. In fact many of these members moved on to countries such as Pakistan, India, Iran, Afghanistan, even China that is where these tribal people are found today.

Those who reject the Torah will be rejected and have no life or kingdom.

The Church Father Clement (Second Century CE) writes the following which may tie up with the Judakon version:

"The Lord has said 'Though you should be joined to me, even in my very bosom and keep not my commandments, I would cast you off, and say to you, 'Depart from me; I know not who you are, you workers of iniquity.'"
(Second Clement 4:5 (or 2:15 in some other editions))

> **Matthew 7:24** Therefore whosoever hears these sayings of mine, and does them, I will liken him to a wise man, that built his Beyth (house) upon a rock:

There are hidden meanings here. Let me explain.

What's a wise man?

You will find this mentioned in Genesis 41:8 THE WORD KHAKHAM. We use these for our elders, who were the wise sages and we say something like our Khakham said such and such...

The word khakam is also attributed to Em Chockmah (the Holy Spirit) who has all the wisdom given to Her from the Father.

Three terms need explanation:
1. Khakham
2. Beyth
3. Evan

First in **Psalm 135:5** To him that by wisdom made the shamayim: for his loving-kindness endures forever.

In Proverbs 3:19 it says YHWH by wisdom has founded the earth...

The second term is the Hebrew word Beyth which means a house. The very first character of Genesis is a raised Hebrew

89

character Bet for a B, which symbolises the House of Abbah YHWH.

3. Jacob mentioned the rock (Evan).

In Genesis 28:18

> **Genesis 28:18** Then Yaqub rose early in the morning, and took the <u>stone</u> [Evan] that he had put at his head, set it up as a pillar, and poured oil on top of it.

Jacob anointed the rock/stone pouring oil on it. Today Hindus do that and this practice they learnt from our forefathers of putting oil on stones for sanctification.

Jacob was at the place that the Temple was to be built in the future.

> **Matthew 7:24** Therefore whosoever hears these sayings of mine, and does them, I will liken him to a wise man, which built his Beyth (house) upon a rock:

Therefore what house is being talked about in Matthew 7:24? It is talking about the Temple. That wherever you are you will bear the testimony of the Temple. Unfortunately it is not what you are taught in Churches. So what is the allegory? To build your life on the <u>foundation of the Torah</u> for which the Temple was well known. Anyone who does not is a foolish man or foolish woman of which you find many in Christendom.

Therefore we must obey the Torah to the best of our abilities and endure to the end.

> **Matthew 24:13** But he that shall endure to the end, the same shall be rescued.

On the other hand Paul's mishmash "grace" is evident in his letters.

Eph 2:8 (KJV) For by <u>grace</u> are ye saved through faith;

90

This message directly contradicts the Torah. However don't expect Christians to figure this out after all this time. This is not a surprise why these people are still in the dark.

Paul did not save anyone. Now you need to decide today who is your Saviour, Paul or Abbah YHWH?

Paul tells you all you need is assent. While rebbe Yeshua tells you assent is not sufficient.

> **Luke 20:35** But they which shall be accounted worthy to obtain that age,

No assent theology with Luke.

You have to be worthy to enter the coming age. The only way you can make yourself worthy is by accepting the contract of the Torah given to Abraham, then Isaac, Jacob and followed by Musa. Without this you are not worthy considering the contract has terms and agreements! No one got away from terms and agreements; it is for those terms and agreements that we are suffering to this day in our exile so why would Christians get an easy ride?

Reciting or saying "I am saved by grace" is utter and sheer nonsense. Christians using the language that "I have a relationship with Christ" is another folly. If you really had a relationship then be like rebbe Yeshua, obey the commandments, guard the Torah but are you? No, not in a hundred years. Then that relationship is nothing but lip service.

> **Isaiah 29: 13** Therefore the sovereign YHWH said, Forasmuch as this **people draw near me** with **their mouth**, and **with their lips do respect me, but have removed their heart far from me**, and their fear toward me is taught by the traditions of men:

Isn't this what Christians are also good at? No Torah whatsoever in their life.

Rebbe Yeshua taught to obey the Torah/LAW, so do it, and do not look at it as some airy fairy statement. We MUST execute the law in our daily lives.

> **Matthew 19:16-17** (HTHS) And, behold, one came and said to him, Rebbe, what Good mitzvoth (deeds) shall I do, that I may have eternal life? 17 And he said to him, Why ask me concerning the good? There is indeed one good, if you want to enter into Life, **Guard and Do the commandments.**

Paul taught the heresy that you can be saved just as a Christian but your works will only be destroyed.

> **1Corinthians 3:13-15** (KJV) Every man's work shall be made manifest: for the day shall declare it, because it shall be revealed by fire; and the fire shall try every man's work of what sort it is. 14 If any man's work abide which he hath built thereupon, he shall receive a reward. 15 If any man's work shall be burned, he shall suffer loss: but **he himself shall be saved**; yet so as by fire.

Rebbe Yeshua taught that you will suffer loss and lose your salvation. What a contrast difference!!!

> **John 15:6** If a man abides not in me**, he is cast forth** as a branch, and is withered; and men gather them, and **cast them into the fire**, and they are burned.

Rebbe Yeshua was clear if you do not do the works of the Father (Torah) you will be cast out, nothing about your works being removed and you being saved but just the opposite of Pauline teachings. You will be cast out and be thrown into the fire. What fire? The Lake of Fire.

Who is the prophet to the gentiles in the Torah?

It was Balaam. Did he not also prophecy the coming of Messiah and how great is Y'sra'el as a people.

Numbers 24:5 How goodly are your tents, O **Yaqub, and your tabernacles**, O Y'sra'el. 17 I shall see him, but not now: I shall behold him, but not near: there shall come a Star out of Yaqub, **and a Sceptre shall rise out of Y'sra'el**, and shall smite the corners of Moab, and destroy all the children of Sheth.

Yet Balaam's end was to be destroyed. Good speech does not win you brownie points in heaven but real Torah works do.

Paul has headed into the same path as Balaam and is the false prophet to the gentiles by his own admission.

Paul or Yahushua? Paul's contradictions continue with such statements...

He keeps calling it the gospel of Christ in the King James Version;

Rom 15:29 (KJV)... I shall come in the fullness of the blessing of the gospel of Christ

1Cor 9:12 (KJV) ...but suffer all things, lest we should hinder the gospel of Christ.

Gal 1:7 (KJV) Which is not another; but there be some that trouble you, and would pervert the gospel of Christ.

Philip 1:27 (KJV) Only let your conversation be as it becometh the gospel of Christ...

Now let us look if rebbe Yeshua called his teachings his gospel or did he preach the Torah.

John 17:4 I have esteemed you on the earth: I have finished the work which **YOU** gave me to do.

Rebbe Yeshua claims that the work he was doing was not his own but His Father's, then by right what did the Father teach? He taught to obey His voice the Torah!

93

Exodus 19:5 Now therefore, if you will indeed, **obey My voice**, and keep My Contract/Agreement, then you shall be a special possession to Me above all people...

John 10:35 (HTHS) If he called them powers, to which the **word of G-d** came, and the scrolls of YHWH cannot be broken;

Word of G-d - Shortcut for Torah.

John 14:21 He that has my commandments [still Torah], and guards and does them, it is he that loves me: and he that loves me shall be loved of my Ab, and I will love him, and will manifest myself to him.

Rebbe Yeshua already clarified he brought nothing new, that the work he was about to do came from the Father, see John 17.4. We are told in the Torah in Exodus 19:9 to obey the voice which is to obey the Torah commandments. So there is no such thing as the "gospel of Christ" that Paul has been branding about. This is the lie fostered on everyone that is involved in a church. You follow a lie and the end result is a misfortune.

So therefore the besorah (gospel) of the kingdom is Torah. The Torah was now being offered to the Lost sheep or those that were removed from Y'sra'el by refusing to obey the Torah. This is the only thing the gospel is and can be.

Revelation 21:14 tells you that there are only twelve assigned apostles, there is no thirteenth apostle which indicates Paul lied.

Paul not only made false claims of his apostleship but complains of being tried as if we are told not to test him while Revelation 2:2 clearly instructs the test is required to reveal false apostles.

1Co 9:1-2 (KJV) Am I not an apostle? am I not free? Have I not seen Jesus Christ our Lord? Are not ye my work in the Lord? If I be not an apostle unto others,

94

yet doubtless I am to you: for the seal of mine apostleship are ye in the Lord.

Paul's lies continue on in other areas too.

He claims none are right-ruling in Romans 3:10 and what a bizarre claim to make.

Let me start counting:

- Noakh called righteous (right-ruling) Gen 7:1.
- Tamar is called right-ruling (Gen 38:6)
- King David called right-ruling (I Sam 24:17)
- Psalm 5:12 says "YHWH will increase the right-ruling." Since according to Paul there is not a single right-ruling man/woman then why would YHWH even give this statement in the Psalm seems to fly in the face of Pauline contradictions.
- Many other Psalms speak about the right-ruling such as Psalm 34:15;19, 21, Ps 35:27; Ps 37:17 and Ps 52:6...
- The Parents of John the Immerser are called Right-ruling in Luke 1:6.

Paul is saluting a Herodian of his own flesh and lineage in ("Romans 16:11 Salute Herodion my kinsman"). However rebbe Yeshua has warned against the leaven of the Herodians.

> **Mark 8:15** And he commanded them, saying, take heed, beware of the leaven of the Pharisees, and of the **leaven of Herodes**.

We also have issues with Pauline teachings such as when he says meat sacrificed to idols is okay as long as the weak brother is not there, while rebbe Yeshua called this the doctrine of Balaam in Rev 2:14. Rebbe Yeshua later condemned it in Rev 2:20. How is it possible then that you have not understood this?

Also note the council in Jerusalem particularly forbid meat from idols in Acts 15:29, this is a Torah prohibition.

95

Galatians 2:3 But neither Teitus (Titus), who was with me, who was a Syrian, he was not compelled to be circumcised:

Here Paulos played the hypocrite by not asking Titus to circumcise immediately, while this should have been done and he called those wrong who in Judaism were demanding that this should be done. One needs to understand we do not circumcise because we feel compelled or not but we do it because it is an order from Abbah YHWH to Abraham that all those of his household and others that will join him must be circumcised. It is an everlasting commandment, no ifs' or buts'. Those who do not want to circumcise can remain in their lawless camps and have no part with Y'sra'el.

Galatians 2:11-14 But when Kefa was come to Antioch, I opposed him to his face, because he was to be blamed. 12 For before those certain ones came from Yaqub, he did eat with the gentiles: but when they had come, he withdrew and separated himself, fearing them which were of the brit-milah (circumcision). 13 And the other Yahudim joined with him; insomuch that Bar'nabah also was carried away with their hypocrisy. 14 But when I saw that they walked not consistently according to the truth of the besorah, I said to Kefa before them all, If you, being a Yahudi, live after the manner of the gentiles, and not as do the Yahudim, why do you compel the gentiles who have joined with Yahudah to live as do the Yahudim?

Paul once again committing slander by writing and admonishing the elders in the letter of Galatians. He thought himself more worthy than Peter, John and even Yaqub (James). Slander is a grievous sin and Paul is also guilty of this sin. The punishment for this sin is no Kingdom. He railed against the elders, to elevate his position while trying to lower them down. He was not just going against three or four individuals but was actually slandering the elders. All those that slander their elders will have no place in the world to come. We learn this from Balaam who tried to curse and slander Y'sra'el, he also has no place in the world to come.

> **Galatians 1:6-8** I marvel that ye are so soon removed from him that called ye into the favour of Messiah to another besorah: 7 Not that there is another; but there are some people that trouble ye, and would pervert the besorah of Messiah. 8 But though we, or a messenger from shamayim, proclaim any other besorah to you than that which we have preached to you, let him be accursed.

This was a veiled attack that Paul did against Peter and the other disciples of rebbe Yeshua since he came into direct conflict with them on methods of teaching. He is indirectly telling you they will be cursed for teaching in their particular method. This is why Paul was giving out contradictory messages and it started creating problems for those who were strict Torah followers. Paul was typically also accused here of slander and tale-bearing both sins identified in the Tanak (Num 14:36, Lev 19:16 and Pro 25:18).

We have to date around 5600 manuscripts of the Greek New Testament writings. However they have variant readings which number in many thousands. These Gentile scribes made many spelling errors, spelling words in Greek incorrectly when they copied out the manuscripts. This does affect doctrine at times too, but few cases however they did take the liberty to change and add texts which they felt was right to do. One example in the text in Mark 1:41 was changed to read "moved with compassion" opposed to "moved with anger". In another example in John 8:4 the Text was added to make it seem like the Torah of YHWH is no more needed which is the story of the adulterous woman.

In a third example text was added in Mark 16:9-20. From this some of you may already know Christians in America handle snakes and think even if they get bit they will survive but instead they have died.

Mark 16:16 He that believes and is immersed shall be rescued; but he that believes not shall be judged. **17** And these signs shall follow them that believe; in my name shall they cast out unclean ruachots (spirits: demons); they shall speak with new tongues; **18** They shall take up serpents; and if they drink any deadly thing, it shall not hurt them; they shall lay hands on the sick, and they shall recover.

Only seven of the Pauline epistles are believed by Scholars to belong to him the rest are likely forgeries in his name. These are Romans, 1 and 2 Corinthians, Galatians, Philippians, 1 Thessalonians and Philemon known as the seven.

There is also 3 Corinthians and a Letter to the Laodiceans that claim his authorship. These some believe to belong to Paul as well.

Even those that belong to Pauline contradict the Torah in many instances e.g. Romans 10:4.

Rom 10:4 (KJ) For Christ *is* the end of the law for righteousness to every one that believeth.

This is in contradiction to the Torah, which says the following:

> **Deut 30:20** (KJV) That thou mayest love the LORD thy G-d, *and* that **thou mayest obey his voice, and that thou mayest cleave unto him**:

Does it not tell us to cleave to YHWH? However many still want to cleave to Paul and his letters raising them up.

So why then are many Christians cleaving to Paul and looking to him for their salvation? Answer in your own time if you are a Christian because you do a disservice to yourself if you do the above.

98

Then there are the other contradictions from the likes of Paul.

The letter of Ephesians is a clever forgery in Paul's name by another editor; it is the same doctrines espoused in the letter of Colossians. Both are forgeries claiming Paul as the author. Neither is of Paul.

This is well known in scholarly circles. A scholar W.G Kummel has argued this is not Paul's and not his theology.

More Pauline contradictions in Galatians;

Gal 5:2 (KJV) Behold, I Paul say unto you, that if ye be circumcised, Christ shall profit you nothing.

Here one can see this has a contradictory text in trying to remove the Torah and its contracts.

So let us assume we remove the circumcision for a second then where does that leave us, contractless without any hope of G-d ever rescuing us.

It means you no longer can be part of the Abrahamic family. It was circumcision that was given in Genesis 17:10 that allowed one to be part of Abraham's family. So now assume Paul tells you that you should not circumcise then that means the only thing that allows you to join Abraham's family can longer be used and this leaves you outside as a gentile trying to look in and you can never be part of Abraham's family.

This is a total fraud even if claimed to be from Paul. Someone was very confused.

If I was looking at these Epistles of Paul I would reject Galatians as not of Paul and neither the book of Romans. It's more likely written by Rome than Paul.

That would leave only 1 and 2 Corinthians, Philippians, 1 Thessalonians and Philemon that could potentially be credited to Paul.

However, they contradict each other as the letter of Philippians teaches Docetism in Phil 2. Docetism is that G-d became human on earth but he was not really human. Philippians 2:6-8 teaches that G-d emptied himself to become a human. This is just Greek Gnostic theology that found its way in the so called letters of Paul and it has no bearing on the Hebrew Scriptures. Marcion was big into this. Marcion cobbled ten of Paul's letters and took the Gospel of Luke to make up his own New Testament removing any references of YHWH in the Hebrew bible which did not favour him. He thought YHWH was too judgmental and wrathful and that the G-d in the Tanak (Old Testament) could not be the G-d in the New Testament.

This is also in the Gnostic gospels such as gospel of Phillips, Second treatise of the Great Seth, apocalypse of Peter, Gospel of Judas, Gospel of Peter and Acts of John.

Now on the Christian front Marcion kind of theologies are still prevalent in Churches today who reject the Torah. Marcion lives on, while YHWH is shunned!!! They don't know who YHWH is but little do these people know they teach Marcion's heresies.

My suggestion is to cleave to YHWH, don't let go of him and His Torah just as He said in Deuteronomy 30:20 or you will die without any salvation. Do not put your faith in the NT as some kind of Panacea; it's not what it is claimed.

> **Yirmeyah 16:19** O YHWH, my strength, and my fortress, and my refuge in the day of affliction, the nations shall come to you from the ends of the earth, and shall say, Surely our ahvot (fathers) have inherited lies,[12] vanity, and things wherein there is no value.

---

[12] It is not one man's job to change the behavior and the lies that Christendom has adopted and they will in majority continue in them until right at the end while some will find complete truth and leave the lies and come into the full light.

100

Yirmeyah 6:16 Thus says YHWH: "Stand in the Ways[13] and look intently, and make inquiry for the ancient paths,[14] where the good way is,[15] and walk[16] in it; then you will find rest[17] for your souls. But they said, `We will not walk in it.'[18]

The only relied and tested path is the path of the Torah that still passes any critical analysis today by any scholar looking into the text. The testimony of Abraham in the Torah lives on and will always be true. If you examine the text of the Tanak and then look at the Dead Sea scrolls the doctrines and teachings of YHWH line up 100 percent.

The manuscripts that we have from Leningrad Codex which is the complete manuscript of the Tanak lines up nicely in every doctrine and teaching in the Dead Sea Scrolls. What does this tell you? That the copies we have of the Tanak is 100% reliable and you can put your life on it. So once again to reiterate a point cleave to YHWH and let go of Paul the self aggrandized apostle.

Go back to the teachings Musa and to love YHWH with all your heart and there you will find rest for your souls. Those of you who don't know YHWH get to know Him it is He who revealed himself to the prophets of old and spoke to them one to one. Those of you who hate coloured people well good luck to you to live on your own and find your own salvation. Those of you who want to know more read my book Yahushua the Black Messiah available from Amazon.

---

[13] The 'WAY,' that Yahushua proclaimed in John 14:6.

[14] The idea behind the Hebrew word is these paths are tried and tested and never failed, meaning Torah is our way to freedom and rescue. The written Torah leads to the speaking Torah Messiah.

[15] Torah

[16] Keep the commandments.

[17] Rescue

[18] Many Christians have said they will not walk in Torah just like Y'sra'el rebelled, Christians have also rebelled.

Conclusion

Last but not least I leave you with some pertinent quotes from history.

Tertullian, "I must approach this inquiry with uneasiness when I find [Paul] affirmed to be an apostle of whom in the list of apostles in the gospel I find no trace."

St Augustine of Hippo, Letter 28, to Jerome (394): I have been reading also some writings ascribed to you, on the Epistles of the Apostle Paul. In reading your exposition of the Epistle to the Galatians,... most disastrous consequences must follow upon our believing that anything false is found in the sacred books: that is to say, that the men by whom the Scripture has been given to us and committed to writing, did put down in these books anything false.... For if you once admit into such a high sanctuary of authority one false statement as made in the way of duty, there will not be left a single sentence of those books which, if appearing to any one difficult in practice or hard to believe, may not by the same fatal rule be explained away, as a statement in which intentionally and under a sense of duty, the author declared what was not true.... If indeed Peter seemed to (Paul) to be doing what was right, and if notwithstanding, he, in order to soothe troublesome opponents, both said and wrote that Peter did what was wrong—if we say thus,... nowhere in the sacred books shall the authority of pure truth stand sure. ●

Letter 40, to Jerome (397): If it be possible for men to say and believe that, after introducing his narrative with these words, 'The things which I write unto you, behold, before G-d, I lie not', the apostle (Paul) lied when he said of Peter and Barnabas, 'I saw that they walked not uprightly, according to the truth of the gospel',... [Then] if they did walk uprightly, Paul wrote what was false; and if he wrote what was false here, when did he say what was true? ● The Harmony of the Gospels, III.25.71 (400): The statement which Paul gives ... runs thus: He was seen of Cephas, then of the twelve: after that He was seen of above five hundred brethren at once. And thus it is not made clear who these twelve were, just as we are not informed who these five hundred were.... For now the apostle might speak of those whom the Lord designated

102

apostles, not as the twelve, but as the eleven. Some codices, indeed, contain this very reading. I take that, however, to be an emendation introduced by men who were perplexed by the text, supposing it to refer to those twelve apostles who, by the time when Judas disappeared, were really only eleven.

St Jerome, Letter 112, to Augustine (404): Porphyry ... accuses Paul of presumption because he dared to reprove Peter and rebuke him to his face, and by reasoning convict him of having done wrong; that is to say, of being in the very fault which he himself, who blamed another for transgressing, had committed.... Oh blessed Apostle Paul—who had rebuked Peter for hypocrisy, because he withdrew himself from the Gentiles through fear of the Jews who came from James—why are you, notwithstanding your own doctrine, compelled to circumcise Timothy (Acts 16:3), the son of a Gentile, nay more, a Gentile himself?

Peter Abelard, Sic et Non (1120): Writing in reply to St. Augustine, after he had been brought to task by Augustine concerning the exposition of a certain spot in Paul's Epistle to the Galatians, Jerome said (Epist.112.4), 'You ask why I have said in my commentary on Paul's letter to the Galatians that Paul could not have rebuked Peter for what he himself had also done. And you asserted that the reproof of the Apostle was not merely feigned, but true guidance, and that I ought not to teach a falsehood. I respond that ... I followed the commentary of Origen.' ● Letters of Direction (before 1142): We know of course that when writing to the Thessalonians the Apostle [Paul] sharply rebuked certain idle busybodies by saying that 'A man who will not work shall not eat.'... But was not Mary sitting idle in order to listen to the words of Christ, while Martha was ... grumbling rather enviously about her sister's repose?

Thomas Paine, The Age of Reason (1794): That manufacturer of quibbles, St. Paul,... [wrote] a collection of letters under the name of epistles.... Out of the matters contained in those books... the church has set up a system of religion very contradictory to the character of the person whose name it bears. It has set up a religion of pomp and of revenue, in

103

pretended imitation of a person whose life was humility and poverty.

Thomas Jefferson, 'Letter to William Short' (1820): Paul was the ... first corrupter of the doctrines of Jesus.

Søren Kierkegaard, Letter to Peter Wilhelm Lund (1.VI.1835): In Christianity itself there are contradictions so great that they prevent an unobstructed view. ● The Journals (1849): In Christ the religious is completely present-tense; in Paul it is already on the way to becoming doctrine. One can imagine the rest!... This trend has been kept up for G-d knows how many centuries. ● (1850) When Jesus Christ lived, he was indeed the prototype.

The task of faith is ... to imitate Christ, become a disciple. Then Christ dies. Now, through the Apostle Paul, comes a basic alteration.... He draws attention away from imitation and fixes it decisively upon the death of Christ the Atoner. ● (1854) What Luther failed to realize is that the true situation is that the Apostle [Paul] has already degenerated by comparison with the Gospel. ● (1855) It becomes the disciple who decides what Christianity is, not the master, not Christ but Paul,... [who] threw Christianity away completely, turning it upside down, getting it to be just the opposite of what it is in the [original] Christian proclamation. ●

For Self-Examination Recommended to the Present Ae, I (1851): 'G-d's Word' is indeed the mirror—but, but—oh, how enormously complicated—strictly speaking, how much belongs to 'G-d's Word'? Which books are authentic? ● 'My Task', The Moment (1.IX.1855): If in the apostle [Paul]'s proclamation there is even the slightest thing that could pertain to what has become the sophistry corruptive of all true Christianity, then I must raise an outcry lest the sophists summarily cite the apostle. It is of great importance ... to correct the enormous confusion Luther caused by inverting the relation and actually criticizing Christ by means of Paul, the Master by means of the follower.... What I have done is to hold Christ's proclamation alongside the apostle's.

104

Adolf von Harnack, History of Dogma, I (1885): The Pauline Gospel is not identical with the original Gospel.... The empty grave on the third day ... is directly excluded by the way in which Paul has portrayed the resurrection (1 Cor. XV).... Paul knows nothing of Ascension.... Every tendency which courageously disregards spurious traditions is compelled to turn to the Pauline Epistles—which, on the one hand, present such a profound type of Christianity, and on the other, darken and narrow the judgment about the preaching of Christ himself.

Mark Twain, Letters from the Earth (1909): Paul ... advised against sexual intercourse altogether. A great change from the divine view. ● Notebooks (date?): If Christ were here now, there is one thing he would not be—a Christian.

Joseph Klausner, Jesus of Nazareth, III.3 (1926): In all Paul's writings we find no reliable historical facts about the life and work of Jesus.... He was not one of Jesus' disciples nor, apparently, had he ever seen him while he was on earth; in the latter event he must have been subservient to James, the brother of Jesus, to Peter and the other Apostles. ● From Jesus to Paul, VI (1943): Saul was the real founder of Christianity as a new religion.... The disciples and brethren of Jesus who were intimate with the crucified Messiah during his lifetime and had received instruction, parables, and promises from his own lips, would reproach Paul in effect thus: You are not a true apostle, and in vain do you on your own authority set aside the ceremonial laws; for you did not attend rebbe Yeshua, you were not intimate with him, and you cannot know his teaching firsthand.... [Regarding] the vision on the road to Damascus... we have here an attack of 'falling sickness' or epilepsy.... We find in him also the characteristics of a thorough melancholic.... There is almost no abusive name which Paul does not give to his opponents. They are 'false brethren', 'false apostles', 'hypocrites' and 'dissemblers'.... The whole 'apostleship' of Paul is based on the 'heavenly vision' which he saw on the road to Damascus.... Paul was far from being a saint.

Rebbe Simon Altaf Hakohen: Those who have taken the Pauline epistles as sacred writ have already fallen from holding sacred the Contracts that YHWH gave our people hence thus they continue in vanity. Paul was not only a false apostle but his doctrines in the form of letters and his diatribes against the disciples of rebbe Yeshua were further corrupted by Rome.

Every book of the New Testament has been tainted and nothing can be trusted out of it anymore.

One such example is as follows:

Paul makes the claim that he was sent to the gentiles and Peter was sent to the Jews yet Peter makes the exact opposite claim about himself proving Paul a liar.

Pauline claim
Galatians 2:7 (KJV) But contrariwise, when they saw that the gospel of the uncircumcision was committed unto me, as the gospel of the circumcision was unto Peter;

> Peter's statement instead
>> **Act 15:7** (KJV) And when there had been much disputing, Peter rose up, and said unto them, Men and brethren, ye know how that a good while ago G-d made choice among us, that **the Gentiles by my mouth should hear the word of the gospel**, and believe.

Contradictions in the same books or with other books.

Paul claims that the law puts you in bondage quoting Galatians 4:25;

> **Galatians 4:25** For this Hagar is Mount Sini'yah (Sinai) in Arabia, and answers to Yerushalim which now is, and is in bondage with her children.

Yet YHWH tells us that He actually brought us out of Bondage (Exo 6:6) so who is telling the truth Moses or Paul?

Exodus 6:6 Therefore say to the children of Y'sra'el, I am YHWH, and I will bring you out from under the burdens of the Mitzrim (Egyptians), and I will rescue you from their bondage, and I will redeem you with an outstretched Arm and with great judgments:

Philippians 2:5-7 Let this mind be in you, which was also in Messiah Yahushua: 6 Who, being in the form of G-d, thought it not robbery to be equal with G-d: 7 But emptied himself, and took upon him the form of a servant, and was made in the likeness of men: 8 And being found in fashion as a man, he humbled himself, and became obedient to death, even the death of the execution stake.

HTHS commentary: Paul's word doubtful of pagan origin. These words which are not inspired contradict. The Roman Catholic Clergy admitted in this error of Paulos in 1951 rejecting this statement as errant and contradictory. These statements of Paulos gave rise to Arianism. Pope Pius XII wrote in his Sempiternus Rex Christus in which he admitted to 'misunderstand' Paul in Philippians 2:7, and stated we cannot allow that to destroy the message of John 1:1. This teaching of the doctrine of kenosis was used by Arius in 306 CE who stated His teaching [that the Son was ontologically inferior to the Father] was a product of Greek rationalism, combined with the teachings of both Arius and Origen. Arius was the first hence why the distancing from Arius. Paulos was a very confused man mixing Greek thinking with Hebrew. Those that raise Paulos to the level of inspired cannot reconcile these statements.

Were these introduced by scribes who were working as part of Rome or was Paul the most confused man on earth at his time? Now this is not a thesis on which is and which is not a genuine saying in the New Testament. Suffice is to say that the King is always Torah and then the Tanak. Anyone or anybody who treats the New Testament any higher is acting in folly.

The Catholic Church admits of forgery of scriptures, that is, what they term to be "scriptures". The Catholic Encyclopaedia, volume 6, which can be viewed online here http://www.ccel.org/ccel/herbermann/cathen06.html admits the following: "Substitution of false documents and tampering with genuine ones was quite a trade in the Middle Ages." "The classical and o t commented text on this matter is the chapter Licet v, "De crimine falsi" in which Innocent III (1198 points out to the bishop and chapter of Milan nine species of forgery which had come under his notice." - In his book, "Forgery in Christianity", Joseph Wheless writes, "Bishop Eusebius of Caesarea, the great "Father of Church History" (324 A.D.) whom Niebuhr terms "a very dishonest writer," -- of which we shall see many notable instances, -- says this: "But it is not our place to describe the sad misfortunes which finally came upon [the Christians], as we do not think it proper, moreover, to, record their divisions and unnatural conduct to each other before the persecution -- [by Diocletian, 305 A.D.]. Wherefore we have decided to relate nothing concerning them except things in which we can vindicate the Divine judgment. ... But we shall introduce into this history in general only those events which may be useful first to ourselves and afterwards to posterity." (Ecclesiastical History, viii, 2; N&PNF. I, 323-324.)"

From the evidence presented, I make the statement that every document of the "New Testament" has been corrupted. Therefore, they cannot be trusted 100% as changes were introduced. We must be very careful what we believe in the NT, and what we put our faith into. I will tell you something, the quotation in 'John 14:6' is also corrupted, but I will leave it at that for you to work out which part of it is corrupted. The letters of 1, 2 and 3 John and I and 2 Peter are forgeries.

This is not to say that we do not have a record of the Aramaic/Hebrew of the gospels. We do have surviving copies of MattithYahu; we have surviving copies of the Aramaic side

108

of the gospels and letters. But, as I have stated, the "New Testament" is not Scripture and not sacred. Do not put your life on it, otherwise you will regret it; if you wish to put your life on something, put it on the Torah, you will never regret it because rebbe Yeshua actually taught Torah before he was deified.

Yes the NT does have the biographies and the sayings of rebbe Yeshua. However none of my forefathers treated the Brit Chadasha or New Testament as sacred writ and did not read it in the Temple and neither will I as a Lewite call them sacred. I am commanded to set-apart the sacred from the secular. The New Testament must be 100% in sync with the Torah and if any of it is not then it cannot be held as reliable. Some verses in the NT are out of sync hence it cannot be held to be 100% reliable text, it has thousands of variant readings. You can make whatever claims you like but can you honestly say the same for the Tanak (the Hebrew bible)?

The Tanak is 100% reliable and was held as sacred by the Temple authorities. So who can throw around his weight? The Temple with its priesthood or the Joe on the street with his Pauline epistles?

Think about how our forefathers functioned which will help you understand what is our theology and what is not.

You can either follow Paul of Tarsus who offers nothing or you can go back to the words of the Rebbe Yeshua and start to diligently follow the Torah so that you are in line with the Contracts given to Y'sra'el as there is no salvation out side of that.

Paul's jealousy and murmuring can be seen in Galatians 1:1 when he complains that he is not chosen by men but rather by the Jesus himself when his diatribe is levelled towards the selection of Matthias instead of him in Acts 1:26 as Matthias was chosen by the council. Paul tries to overrule the council by suggesting he was selected from above. If he was selected from above then how come they did not pick his name versus Matthias?

> **Galatians 1:1** Paulos, an Emissary, (not of men, neither by man, but by Yahushua, and Ab YHWH, who raised him from the dead;)

Note Pauline claims to be from above and not below.

> Acts 1:26 And then they cast lots; and the one chosen was Mattityahu; and he was numbered with the eleven Emissaries.

Paul claimed to be an apostle sixteen times in his letters and when he was faced with king Agrippa he never mentioned himself as an apostle but instead made himself this time only to be a minister and witness. Why did he give contradictory statements?

> **2Co 12:7 (KJV)** And lest I should be exalted above measure through the abundance of the revelations, there was given to me a thorn in the flesh, the messenger of Satan to buffet me, lest I should be exalted above measure.

Only the unwise can believe in such contradictory statements;

As can be seen Paul had some weird ideas that Satan can buffet believers while we are actually rescued out of every Satanic plot but he seems to think he was being kept humble.

This is nothing but a total lie. Now that you have been shown the ill choice of following Paul it's up to you whether you turn away from such men of deceit or you continue with them to the detriment of your salvation /rescue.

Shalom Shalom

May the El of Y'sra'el guide you and increase those of you who obey Him.

Rabbi Simon Altaf HaKohen

I leave you with the rebbe's statement;

Matthew 28:19-20
19 לכו אתם
20 ולמדו אותם לקיים כל הדברים
אשר ציויתי אתכם עד עולם

19 Go to them
20 And teaching them to Guard and Do all the words of
the Commandments as a witness forever.

May the El of Y'sra'el guide you and increase those of you
who obey His Torah.
Rabbi Simon Altaf Hakohen
For groundbreaking articles... www.african-israel.com.
**TRUTH UNLEASHED BUT CAN YOU HANDLE
IT?**
This article may be distributed freely without alteration
and is copyright to African-Israel Union of International
Qahalim.
For further questions either call or write to
africanysrael@yahoo.com.
For USA; African-Israel,8111 Mainland, Suite 104-152,
San Antonio, Texas, 78240, USA Tel 1-210-827-3907
For contact with Rebbe Simon Altaf Hakohen email
shimoun63@yahoo.com
We hope this article has given you an increase. Please
write to us and let us know if this has been a help to you
and if you have any other questions or come and join us in
our weekly Paltalk teachings every Shabbat 9am central
time/3pm UK time under the category of Judaism called
Israel in the nations Torah Guardians.
www.african-israel.com/paltalk.html
Send the mail to africanysrael@yahoo.com. For prophecy
books and DVDs that will help many understand the
Bible more. Visit www.african-Israel.com or
www.israelfound.com.
For youtube teachings please go to
www.youtube.com/simalt.

111

Our youtube channel: www.youtube.com/simalt
Paltalk: The Observers of the Real Yahushua and Torah on Saturday 10am central time, 3pm UK time.
For books
http://www.african-israel.com/Books/books.html
For videos...
www.lulu.com/simalt
The Hidden Truths Hebraic Scrolls Complete Bible can be ordered at the URL below. www.african-israel.com. Note the excellent translation of bible which reflects our mission to Africa and the true genetic Hebrews mentioned in the bible who live in the western word such as in Europe, Americas and in the Caribbean islands including many other countries like Brazil, India, Iran and Pakistan. They were taken into Brazil by the Sephardic (Jews – Gentile converts into Judaism) a prophecy fulfilled in the Bible.

We suggest you visit our website to see the following Titles:
www.african-israel.com
All these books are available from www.Amazon.com

Beyth Yahushua – the Son of Tzadok, the Son of Dawud
Would you like to know the identity of Yahushua's family, the man many call Jesus? Did He have brothers and sisters, did He get married, and are not Rabbis meant to marry?

Is it true if Mary Magdalene was His wife and if not then what relationship did she have with him?

Are you fed-up of hearing objections from unbelievers such as "since you do not know who Matthew, Mark, Luke and John were then how can you claim to have the truth?" Now you will know the truth without asking your pastor.

Who was Nicodemus and what relationship did Jesus have with Nicodemus? Who was the wider family of Jesus of Nazareth?

Was he a wandering Jew with no belongings and no family and living outside his home with women offering him money and food? This picture is both misleading and deceptive.

Do you want to know the powerful family of rebbe Yahushua that was a threat to Rome?

Who were Mark, Luke, and Matthew? Was Luke a gentile or a Hebrew priest?

What about the genealogy of Luke and Matthew in which the two fathers of Yahushua mentioned are Heli or Jacob in Matthew chapter 1:16 and Luke chapter 3:23 respectively?

This book will give you new insights and the rich history of Yahushua's family.

Islam, Peace or Beast
Have you ever wondered why radical Muslims are blowing up buildings, bombings planes and creating havoc? We illustrate in this book the reality of radical Islam and the end of days that are upon us. Why are our governments reluctant to tell us the truth we uncover many details. Does the Bible reference Middle-Eastern nations or European nations, how many verses can you spot for Europe? Are Muslims just maligned or what we see in Iraq today is what was spoken about in Isaiah 13 and Isaiah 14? The jihad crazed mind, Rev 17, the beast that arose out of the desert, the beheadings now on a TV in front of you myth or reality.
Does the prophet Ezekiel confirm the end is with Islamists or Europeans? Your eyes are about to be opened on a story that began back in Genesis 4000 years ago.

113

World War III – Unmasking the End-Times Beast
Who is the Antichrist, what countries are aligned with him and many of your other questions answered. All revealed in this book. Which might be the ten nations of the Antichrist? What did the prophets say on these events? Is the Anti-Messiah a Jew? Where is Babylon and the daughter of Babylon in 2015. The true epic battle for Jerusalem. What part will the United States and United Kingdom play in the End of Days. See how accurate Rabbi Simon predicts the coming together of these nations. What are the ships of Kittim, who is Ararat, Minni and Ashkenaz? Who are the two thirds of people that will be killed? Is it the whole world, a single country or a single geographic location?

World War III – Salvation of the Jews
- How will the salvation of the Jews come about, will they convert to Christianity or will Christianity be folded into Judaism?
- Will the 3rd Temple be built before the coming of the future Messiah? Where is the real site of the Third Temple? Analyzed and explained with the correct hermeneutics.
- Will we have a war with Iran and when? Considering the pundits have been wrong since the last 10 years and only Rabbi Simon has been on track up to this time. What signs will absolutely indicate impending war with Iran calculated and revealed.
- When will the Messiah come, what signs should we be looking for, is it on a Jubilee year?
- Will the Messiah come on the feast of Trumpets fact or fiction?
- Will America win the war in Afghanistan? Yes and No answer with details.
- Who is the prince of Ezekiel and why is he making sin sacrifices. Can one call these educational as Christians do? Read the correct answers...

114

- Should we support the Jewish Aliyah to Israel under a secular government? Who are the real Children of Israel?

Rabbi Simon is the only Rabbi to look at the thorny issues that no one has addressed to date while many people mostly run with popular opinions coloured by bad theology by picking and choosing verses in isolation. Is modern Zionism biblical? Is Israel right to take over territories occupied by Palestinians today? Should people be selling up homes to go and live in Israel? All these thorny questions and even more answered in this book the sequel to the popular prophecy book World War III - Unmasking the End-Times Beast.

Dear Muslim – Meet YHWH the Elohim of Abraham
Truth explained, best seller step by step detailing and unveiling Islam! This book is designed for that friend, son or daughter who is about to convert into Islam but needs to read this first. This is the <u>one</u> stop to saving their soul. Don't procrastinate, get it today so that they may see what is the truth before they cause themselves to be confounded and duped into something totally not true.

The Feasts of YHWH, the Elohim of Israel
Have you ever asked why the feasts were given to Israel as a people? What is the meaning of the festivals and what about their purpose which is all explained in this detailed book that delves into the signs and the fulfillment of the feasts. Why are we to obey the feasts <u>forever</u> and if we do not then we could potentially lose our place in the kingdom entry! Well no one said that before but now you will see and experience an exhilarating experience of knowing what it is like to be there. How does it feel to be up all night to celebrate the festival of Shavuot (Pentecost), what does it mean and many other details.

Testament of Abraham
Now it's time to hear Abraham's story from his own mouth what happened, how did he become Elohim's friend. What other missing information that we are not

115

told about is made available. Without Abraham there will be no Judaism, no Islam and no Christianity. He is the pivotal point upon which all three religious text claim right but who does Abraham really belong to?

What is Truth?
Have you wondered what truth is and how we measure it? How do we arrive at the conclusion that what you have is truth? How do you know that the religion you have been following for so many years is the original faith? Can we examine Atheism and say why it is or is not true, what about Christianity? We examine these things.

Hidden Truths Hebraic Scrolls Study Bible 5th Edition (Complete)

The HT Complete Bible more myths busted. Over 1300 pages packed absolutely full of information - no Hebrew roots Bible even comes close this is guaranteed and these scrolls are the difference between night and day, see for yourself!!! The politically incorrect guide to the Elohim of Israel and the real chosen people of YHWH. Are you willing to listen to what YHWH has said about our world and how He is going to restore all things back including His real chosen people hidden to this day?

Many texts uncovered and explained in great details accurately and many corrections made to the many faulty translations out there making this a real eye-opener text.

➔ Was Chava (Eve) the only woman in the garden? We reveal a deep held secret.
➔ Where did the demons come from?
➔ Ezekiel refers to some of Israel's evil deeds in Egypt explicitly uncovered which are glossed over in the King James Version.
➔ Who are the Real Hebrews of the Bible, which people does the land of Y'sra'el really belong to? Time to do away with the deception.
➔ Did Abraham keep the Sabbath? We show you when and where.
➔ But I thought Keturah was Hagar, another error of Judaism corrected.
➔ But I thought Keturah was married to Abraham after Sarah's death, no not really. A very bad textual translation in Genesis 25:1.
➔ Who was Balaam, a profit for cash as are many pastors and Bishops today doing the same thing running and chasing after the Almighty dollar?
➔ Who were Abraham's ancestors, Africans or Europeans?
➔ Why did Isaac marry at forty years of age, what happened to his first wife? Rebecca was not his only wife, an error and ignorance of Christendom exposed?

117

- → Where is Noah's ark likely to be? Not Ararat in Turkey or Iran another error.
- → Who are the four wives of Abraham and who is the real firstborn? Not Ishmael and not even Isaac. Was Isaac his only begotten son another error?
- → All the modification of modern Judaism of the scribes has been undone to give you what was the real text including the original conversation of the Serpent with Chava (Gen 3) unedited plus Abraham's conversation unedited at last in Genesis 18.

The legendary Rabbi Simon Altaf guarantees that this will teach you to take the best out there and open their eyes in prophecy, historical argument and theology. He will personally mentor you through the texts of the Torah, the prophets. Does any Bible seller offer this extent of training? We do. And Rabbi Simon is available at the end of an e-mail. We do not charge for our calls or any teachings or advise over the phone.

Sefer Yashar (The Book of Jasher)
The book of Yashar has been translated from the original sources and with added commentary, corrected names of Elohim with the sacred names and with other missing text from the Hebrew. This will add to the gaps in your knowledge from the book of Genesis such as the following:
- What did the wicked do before the flood?
- Who were Abraham's African ancestors?
- Did Abraham have two wives?
- What relationship did Abraham have with Eli'ezer?
- Did Isaac wait forty years to be married?
- Why did Sarah die so suddenly?
- Did Moses marry in Egypt?
- Moses, what colour? White or Black.
- Many other questions now answered.

Seferim Chanoch (The Books of Enoch)

118

The books of Enoch details the fall, the names of the angels, what happened in the beginning and what was the result of those fallen angels. Where are they now and what will happen to them. He also reveals the birth of Noach and some very important details around this about the African ancestry of the patriarchs. He reveals the Son of Elohim. And many other important details to complete your knowledge.

Yahushua – The Black Messiah
Have you been lied to about the true identity of Yahushua? Have you been shown pictures of the idolatrous Borgia Cesare and may have believed that this Caucasian hybrid was the one Christians believe to be Messiah? What ethnicity was rebbe Jesus and what race of people did He belong to? Is it important that we know His ethnicity? What colour was Moses, King David and King Solomon? We examine and look at the massive fraud perpetrated upon the western nations by their leaders to hide the real identity of the true Hebrew Israelite people and race which are being restored in these Last Days. Rebbe Yahushua said everything will be restored and that includes His and His people's ethnicity and colour. Would you like to know because it affects your eternity and His true message then get this book now.

Hebrew Wisdom – Kabbalah
The book's purpose is to illustrate basic principles of Kabbalah and to reveal some of the Kabbalah symbolisms. We look at the Sefirots what they mean and how they apply in the Tanak. We also look at the first chapter in Genesis and examine some of the symbols there. We examine the name of Elohim in Exodus 3:14 and see what it means. This book also demonstrates the application of Kabbalah.

We also reveal the Merkabah in Ezekiel Chapter 1 and how it relates to the Messiah. This book will be a real eye opener for many. We also give you a kabbalistic technique that can give you the ability to protect your family and your finances.

The Apocrypha (With Pirke Avot 'Ethics of The Fathers')

Read the fifteen books of the Apocrypha to get an understanding of the events both of the exile and of Israel's early history. Read Ethics of the Fathers to understand rabbinic wisdom and some important elements of the story of Genesis. The tests, the trials and the miracles of the Temples. Without these books the story in the bible is incomplete and has gaps which these books will fill up and give you a more complete understanding.

African-Israel Siddur transliterated Hebrew with English (Daily life prayers)

Many times we wonder what prayers should we do when we go to bed, when we leave our home in the morning and how do we pray daily? What prayer should I do if I have a ritual bath? What prayer is for affixing a Mezuzah? Each year you wonder how to do the Passover Aggadah and what is the procedure. This book also covers women's niddah laws to give you understanding into women's ritual purity. Unlike other prayer books Rabbi Simon actually bothers to explain small details that are important and often ignored. What do you do when a relative dies, what prayers do you do at graveyards, how to celebrate the death of loved one's? Can you do prayers for the dead? This is one book you should not be without.

World War III, The Second Exodus, Y'sra'el's return journey home

How will the genetic Hebrews be taken back to the land? Are the present day Jews in Y'sra'el of ancient stock? Is there any prophecy of foreigners invading Y'sra'el and inhabiting the land? How will Elohim have war with Amalek and wipe them out and who is Amalek today? Why is the Church so confused about bible prophecy?

How will the end come and why is the world hiding the identity of the true Y'sra'elites? Will there be a rapture or marching back on foot? What happens if we die in our exile? And many more questions answered. The time has come to expose the errors of others.

What Else Have They Kept From Us?
This book is as the result of an e-mail conversation with a person who asked me some questions and one of her questions upon my answer was "What else have they kept from us?" This was the question that led to this book because instead of answering people with small sections of answers, I decided the time had come that a book had to be written to answer and address everything as it happened from the start to the end so that many may see that the deception is real and it's a deep cunning deception which starts from your TV screens, in your newspapers followed by wherever you go in your daily life.

How would a person know that they are being deceived if they do not know what to look for? Its like a Ten Pound note well if you saw the original then you have something to compare the false note with but what if you were never presented with the original and always had the fake in your pocket then you will likely think the fake is real and this is how it is with Christianity today that is simply mixing paganism with truth. A false Ten pound note or a bad tender which will give you no value when you redeem it as I uncover it in the pages of this book. Who was Yahushua, the real Hebrews and Y'sra'el.

Patriarchal Marriage, Y'sra'el's Right-Ruling Way of Life, Methods and Practice
How did the Y'sra'elites live? What form of marriage did they practice and how did they practice it? This book is about to show you what was Elohim's design from the beginning and how the Y'sra'elites lived within Elohim's required parameters. Today these things appear mythological but here we show you the methods and

ways of how this lifestyle was practiced and is being restored in these last days while the much touted monogamy is wrecking lives and destroying families and society around us. How many marriages are breaking down as a result of the wrong model and how many children are living fatherless lives while women live husbandless and unfulfilled lives. This book will show you why the Greek and Roman monogamy model with a husband and a wife and a bit on the side does not work. While Elohim's model of plural marriage with Torah monogamy is an everlasting model that not only works but saves many children from losing their father's and women from losing good husbands.

The Scroll of Yahubel (Jubilees)
The information that is missing in the Torah has been put in here to aid us in understanding the book of Genesis more. There are gaps in Genesis with what happened with Noakh? What was going on in Moses's time? This scroll allows us to piece together that information that is so important for our understanding. True names edition with many corrections made.

Who am I?
A Children's book to help the black Hebrew children with identity and direction in life. Many Hebrew children while looking for identity easily stray. While they search for love they end up in gangs to prove themselves and search for that missing something. When they do not find love in their homes due to broken homes often venturing out with devastating consequences, getting involved in criminal activities to prove themselves ruining their lives. This book's purpose is to help these children and even adults find themselves to teach them who they are and to find sound direction in life to secure you to the Elohim of our ancestors where you belong. This will help change many lives.

Paul of Tarsus - The Thirteenth Apostle

We examine if Paul is an apostle and if Pauline epistles match teachings out of the Torah and with the sayings of the Messiah Yahushua. We also show you what the Catholic Church has been hiding from you. You may be surprised to learn that things are not what they seem and you may have been deceived all this time. It's time for the deception to lift and for you to return to the ancient paths.

Hidden Truths Hebraic Scrolls Compendium Guide - For those who have the Hidden-Truths Hebraic Scrolls this is a must buy to give you a deeper understanding under the text and its meaning where the footnotes are expounded upon further in various books of the scrolls.

Hebrew Characters, The Power to have prayers answered
Have you ever tried praying and find that either your prayers take very long time to answer or they don't get answered at all? In frustration you ask other friends to pray for you in hope that you may get an answer from G-d soon.
I have given considerable thought about the condition of our people and how many languish in poverty, in situations where they seek for help because they are given false dogmas, put in religious bondage and slavery of the mind and heart.

Many times they make their own lives harder because they have spent so much time in the nations that they just want to live like the gentiles and not Hebrew as they are unaware how to benefit themselves that await them. I know it can be a lonely road at times. Our Abbah in the heavens feels our pain while we live in exile He sends the Em Chomah to be with us. He longs for us to return back to the contracts that we may receive all the increases and benefits that are only meant for us.

However we pass our life by with this that and the other person who gives us no joy but we think maybe if we carry on suffering things will change for the better but

123

things NEVER change. This book was written to help for a time such as this to better the lives of our people. To empower them with the right petitions to give them benefits and increases in employment, love, marriage and sickness. This will help you break the spells of witchcraft, dealing with jealous people around you and personal anger issues. This will help you deal with demonic presences in your homes. This will show you how to receive a timely answer to all your prayers. I have used these methods for my students all over the world which have proven successful for them and have greatly benefited them.

It takes many generations for a right-ruling priest to be born in our generations. How many generations our people have suffered the scourge of the curses for not obeying the Torah? Many are still suffering. The Most High is going to raise his priests one by one until we get our restoration complete. Rabbi Simon is of the priestly family born to help his people.

The Kohen is meant to be a benefit to the people of Y'sra'el and is one of the person's that has been given the authority to stand between the heavenly court and the earthly realm. Christian clergy has been lying to you for so long that you don't know what is good for you anymore. The Melekzadek priest's job is not to stand between the heaven and earth as you have been wrongly taught, his job is to be a King and serve justice on the earth with the Torah. While the Christian clergy teaches everyone can be Melekzadek this is not the truth. Only the Kings of Israel can right hold that title, its not for anyone else.

There is only one everlasting priesthood and that is the Lewitical one. This book has been written by a Lewitical priest of Beyth of Tzadok, its time you reap the benefits so decide wisely. Even if you are a gentile looking to become part of Israel by conversion the opportunity is open to you to obey the Torah.

I want you all to benefit and to receive what rightly belongs to you.

This book for $100 a piece because everything in this manual would forever change your life once you put it in practice but I decided not to do that as my purpose was not that.

However this book is kept at a low price not for $100, no, not even $50 but for a price of $27 only this will forever change the way you think and pray. I am practically giving this away for you to better your lives. The rest is up to you.

New releases for 2015-2017
Ancient Hebrew – Functions, Methods and Meanings. Where did we go wrong?

Religious Confusion and the Everlasting Path to Torah
All the myriads of religious denominations and religious quagmire out there and why the paths of the Torah are the only paths to success and happiness with everlasting life.